T0413848

Human Trafficking

In the post-Cold War era, economic globalization has resulted in the buying and selling of human beings. Poverty, social instability, lawlessness, gender biases, and ethnic hostility have entrapped millions in the world of modern day slavery, with the result that human trafficking is one of the fastest growing criminal industries in the world. Every year, men, women, and children from across the globe are transported within or across borders for the purpose of forced labor and sexual exploitation. Despite the plethora of journalistic articles written on human trafficking there is a need for more rigorous academic analysis of the phenomenon.

Although groups from many different ideologies have embraced policies to end human trafficking, there are still many gaps and unanswered questions, particularly with regard to the amount of, and nature of, the phenomenon. This book provides an insight into the complexity of human trafficking by addressing both how the scope of globalization impacts the sex industry and forced labor, and how vulnerability is a growing cause of human trafficking, affecting traditional diasporic and migratory patterns.

This book was originally published as a special issue of the *Journal of Intercultural Studies*.

Natividad Gutiérrez Chong is a Research Professor at the National Autonomous University of Mexico, Mexico City, Mexico. She holds an MSc and PhD from the London School of Economics and Political Science, UK. She has coordinated several national and international projects related to ethnicity and nationalisms in Latin America and China. She is currently researching ethnic conflicts, trafficking, racism, and gender.

Jenny Bryson Clark is Associate Professor of Political Science and Women's Studies Chair at South Texas College, McAllen, Texas, USA. For the last ten years, she has been actively involved in researching human trafficking and has been creating awareness about trafficking through organizing annual international conferences. She is currently conducting research on gender inequality and trafficking in India.

Human Trafficking

A complex phenomenon of globalization
and vulnerability

Edited by
**Natividad Gutiérrez Chong and
Jenny Bryson Clark**

Routledge
Taylor & Francis Group

LONDON AND NEW YORK

First published 2016
by Routledge
2 Park Square, Milton Park, Abingdon, Oxon, OX14 4RN, UK

and by Routledge
711 Third Avenue, New York, NY 10017, USA

Routledge is an imprint of the Taylor & Francis Group, an informa business

British Library Cataloguing in Publication Data
A catalogue record for this book is available from the British Library

ISBN 13: 978-1-138-94347-6

Typeset in Minion
by RefineCatch Limited, Bungay, Suffolk

Publisher's Note
The publisher accepts responsibility for any inconsistencies that may have
arisen during the conversion of this book from journal articles to book chapters,
namely the possible inclusion of journal terminology.

Disclaimer
Every effort has been made to contact copyright holders for their permission to
reprint material in this book. The publishers would be grateful to hear from any
copyright holder who is not here acknowledged and will undertake to rectify
any errors or omissions in future editions of this book.

Contents

Citation Information

The following chapters were originally published in the *Journal of Intercultural Studies*, volume 35, issue 2 (April 2014). When citing this material, please use the original page numbering for each article, as follows:

Introduction
Trafficking in Persons
Natividad Gutiérrez Chong & Jenny Bryson Clark
Journal of Intercultural Studies, volume 35, issue 2 (April 2014) pp. 123–127

Chapter 2
The Political and Economic Transition from Communism and the Global Sex Trafficking Crisis: A Case Study of Moldova
Jenny Bryson Clark & Denese McArthur
Journal of Intercultural Studies, volume 35, issue 2 (April 2014) pp. 128–144

Chapter 3
Vulnerability to Human Trafficking among the Roma Population in Serbia: The Role of Social Exclusion and Marginalization
Sasha Poucki & Nicole Bryan
Journal of Intercultural Studies, volume 35, issue 2 (April 2014) pp. 145–162

Chapter 4
Sex Trafficking and the Sex Trade Industry: The Processes and Experiences of Nepali Women
Shobha Hamal Gurung
Journal of Intercultural Studies, volume 35, issue 2 (April 2014) pp. 163–181

Chapter 5
Sexual Exploitation and Trafficking of Women and Girls in Mexico: An Analysis on Impact of Violence on Health Status
Arun Kumar Acharya
Journal of Intercultural Studies, volume 35, issue 2 (April 2014) pp. 182–195

CITATION INFORMATION

Chapter 7

Human Trafficking and Sex Industry: Does Ethnicity and Race Matter?
Natividad Gutiérrez Chong
Journal of Intercultural Studies, volume 35, issue 2 (April 2014) pp. 196–213

The following chapter was originally published in the *Journal of Intercultural Studies*, volume 34, issue 2 (April 2013). When citing this material, please use the original page numbering for each article, as follows:

Chapter 1

The Forces Driving Global Migration
Stephen Castles
Journal of Intercultural Studies, volume 34, issue 2 (April 2013) pp. 122–140

The following chapter was originally published in the *Journal of Intercultural Studies*, volume 33, issue 1 (February 2012). When citing this material, please use the original page numbering for each article, as follows:

Chapter 6

The Forgotten Family: Labour Migration and the Collapse of Traditional Values in Thailand's Tribal Communities
Scott Downman
Journal of Intercultural Studies, volume 33, issue 1 (February 2012) pp. 53–68

For any permission-related enquiries please visit:
http://www.tandfonline.com/page/help/permissions

Notes on Contributors

Arun Kumar Acharya holds a PhD in Anthropology from the National Autonomous University of Mexico, Mexico City, Mexico, and a master's degree in Population Studies from the International Institute of Population Studies, Mumbai, India. He is currently working as a Senior Researcher at Instituto de Investigaciones Sociales, UANL, Monterrey, Mexico. He has published 50 scientific articles on migration, gender issues, and trafficking in persons. He has also published three books on migration and trafficking issues in Mexico.

Nicole Bryan is Assistant Professor of Management and International Business at Montclair State University, New Jersey, USA. Her interests include globalization, ethics, and corporate responsibility, with a particular focus on human trafficking, child labour, and forced labour. Her recent fieldwork includes an in-depth study of the motivations for reconciliation and post-conflict transformation within former Yugoslavia. She teaches courses on business ethics, corporate responsibility, and human rights. Currently, she is researching the role of technology in human trafficking as part of a grant from Microsoft and is engaged in research on child labour and forced labour in agriculture.

Stephen Castles is a Research Professor of Sociology at the University of Sydney, Australia, and a Research Associate at the International Migration Institute, University of Oxford, UK. He works on international migration dynamics, social transformation, and migration and development. His recent books include: *The Age of Migration: International Population Movements in the Modern World* (4th Edition, with Mark Miller, 2009); *Migration and Development: Perspectives from the South* (edited with Raúl Delgado Wise, 2008); and *Migration, Citizenship and the European Welfare State: A European Dilemma* (with Carl-Ulrik Schierup and Peo Hansen, 2006).

Natividad Gutiérrez Chong is a Research Professor at the National Autonomous University of Mexico, Mexico City, Mexico. She holds an MSc and PhD from the London School of Economics and Political Science, UK. She has coordinated several national and international projects related to ethnicity and nationalisms in Latin America and China. She is currently researching ethnic conflicts, trafficking, racism, and gender.

Jenny Bryson Clark is Associate Professor of Political Science and Women's Studies Chair at South Texas College, McAllen, Texas, USA. For the last ten years, she has been actively involved in researching human trafficking and has been creating awareness about trafficking through organizing annual international conferences. She is currently conducting research on gender inequality and trafficking in India.

Scott Downman is a journalist and Lecturer in Journalism and Public Relations at Griffith University, Brisbane, Australia. He has served as a community development worker in Thailand with NGOs, including TEAR Australia. Most recently he has worked extensively in village-based projects aimed at combating exploitation among Thailand's ethnic minority communities.

Shobha Hamal Gurung is Assistant Professor of Sociology in the Department of History, Sociology, and Anthropology at Southern Utah University, Cedar City, Utah, USA. She is also a core faculty member of the Women and Gender Studies Program, and the Program Director of the Nepal Summer Study Abroad Program. Her areas of work, teaching, and research include gender, labour, and migration; intersectionality; globalization and transnational studies; sex trafficking, South Asia, and international studies; social justice and human rights. Selected publications include: 'Shifting Gender Roles and Shifting Power Relations: Immigrant/Migrant Nepali Families in New York and Los Angeles' (*Migration, Diaspora and Identity: Cross-National Experiences*, 2014) and 'Gendered Labour: Experiences of Nepali Women within Pan-Ethnic Informal Labour Markets in Boston and New York' (with B. Purkayastha, *Immigrant Workers: In the Neoliberal Age*, 2013).

Denese McArthur is Associate Professor of Government at Tarrant County College in Arlington, Texas, USA. Her current research interests include human trafficking, economic development, and agent-based modelling.

Sasha Poucki is a Research Fellow and Visiting Professor of Management and International Business at Montclair State University, New Jersey, USA. His interests include globalization, transnational crime, and corporate responsibility, with a particular focus on child labour, forced labour, the root causes of human trafficking, and the vulnerability of minority groups. His research on human trafficking includes a study of the Roma in Serbia, Devadasis in India, and Badi in Nepal. Currently, he is researching the role of technology in human trafficking as part of a grant from Microsoft, and is engaged in research on child labour and forced labour in agriculture.

Introduction: Trafficking in Persons

Natividad Gutiérrez Chong & Jenny Bryson Clark

In the last 20 years, human trafficking has become a global problem of unforeseen proportions. Human trafficking affects every country in the world, regardless of socioeconomic status, history, or political structure and most countries are a source, transit, and destination for victims of human trafficking. It is an abhorrent crime of which many of the victims are from the developing and transitional nations. The profits from human trafficking are immense and the United Nations Office of Drugs and Crime places human trafficking as the fastest growing and second most profitable form of transnational crime. The trafficking in human beings is one of the greatest criminal phenomena facing the international community today.

At the same time as human trafficking has grown to significant proportions, much interest has also been generated on the subject. The struggle to understand human trafficking, however, has been hampered by the lack of common terminology and a conceptual framework for discussing the problem. There is no consistent use of the term *human trafficking* and little consensus on what the term encompasses. Many associate human trafficking with forced prostitution and fail to take into consideration exploitation in other sectors such as agriculture, manufacturing, construction, hotel industry, and domestic service. As human trafficking and migrant smuggling are intimately connected, there is still confusion between the two and it is easy for human trafficking to disappear behind migrant smuggling, which is much more pervasive and politically salient.

Human trafficking is complex and the clandestine nature of the phenomenon makes estimating the numbers of people trafficked difficult. Many government estimates of the number of trafficked persons are dubious at best. Despite the disparities in data, there is consensus among governments, academics, and practitioners that the scale is significant and of deep concern. Conservative estimates suggest that at least 2.5 million women, children, and men are lured or forced across international borders (transnational human trafficking) every year and a significant amount more are trafficked within borders (internal human trafficking) forced to work against their will often in unsafe deplorable conditions.

The international community attempted to address human trafficking in 2000, when the United Nations adopted protocols to address human smuggling and human trafficking along with the United Nations Convention on Transnational Crime. Article 3a of the protocol to prevent, suppress and punish trafficking in persons defines human trafficking as:

> The recruitment, transportation, transfer, harbouring or receipt of persons, by means of threat or use of force or other forms of coercion, of abduction, of fraud, of deception, of the abuse of power or of a position of vulnerability or of the giving or receiving of payments or benefits to achieve the consent of a person having control over another person, for the purpose of exploitation. Exploitation shall include, at a minimum, the exploitation of prostitution or other forms of sexual exploitation, forced labor or services, slavery or practice similar to slavery, servitude or the removal of organs. (UN. Protocol to Suppress and Punish Trafficking in Persons 2000)

Trafficking is identified by the protocol as the action of taking control of another person for the purposes of exploitation, with the means of control ranging from force, or some form of deceit to payment in exchange for consent. While the protocol clearly delineates human trafficking from migrant smuggling in practice, the two are so intimately connected that distinctions are still blurred. Many migrants, particularly women and children, may start off in a consensual agreement by paying a smuggler, but become a trafficking victim.

Apart from the United Nations Conventions, the EU Council in 2002 adopted the Framework Decision on Combating Trafficking in Human Beings. A few years later, the Council of Europe Convention on Against Trafficking in Human Beings was adopted in 2005 and eventually went into force in 2008. In the late 1990s, human trafficking became a concern to the USA and culminated in the passage of the Trafficking Victims Protection Act (TVPA) signed into law on 16 October 2000. Subsequently, many other countries have since adopted legislation on human trafficking.

Globalization, with its accelerating flow of products, and people within an expanding world economy have been a huge impetus for human trafficking. The economic and demographic disparities between the developing and developed nations caused by globalization, free trade, greater economic competition, and a decline of state intervention in the economy have all contributed to the marginalization and impoverishment of countless numbers of people. Structural adjustment and austerity programs imposed on many nations have compounded the problem with people plummeting further from relative poverty to absolute poverty. Structural poverty has resulted in increased movements across borders and increased internal migration from rural areas to urban centers. In response to increased migration, governments have imposed stricter immigration policies leaving many migrants vulnerable to exploitation by traffickers, a common theme running through all the articles in this issue. Despite the international community and governments attempting to address the phenomenon of human trafficking, many challenges remain and the need for more research is pressing. Efforts to combat trafficking remain woefully inadequate and trafficking is poorly understood.

Human trafficking is a complex phenomenon with multiple factors that operate simultaneously. Numerous root causes have been identified for human trafficking. Known as the push factors, they include poverty, corruption, gender, ethnic and racial discrimination, and political instability. In effect, ethnicity, race, national belonging, stereotypes and prejudices, cultural patterns, traditional patriarchal culture, among others, are highlighted as the focus of this special issue, accounting for the exposure of women and children to trafficking.

The vulnerability of women and children resonates in all the articles here. Women and children are disproportionately apt to pay the costs of economic dislocations in their countries and be victims of poverty. The dismantling of many social safety nets in the former Soviet Union has increased burdens on many women and children. With no protections from their own governments they become easy prey for transnational traffickers. Moldova, one of the poorest countries in the region, is a prime example. Moldova has emerged as a source country with women trafficked into Western Europe, Eastern Gulf countries and Turkey, and Russia as outlined in the article by Jennifer Bryson Clark. Another case showing how vulnerability provides a fertile ground for trafficking is the Roma people in Serbia. There is a link between traditional patriarchal culture, stereotypes, prejudices, and social exclusion which push Roma people into trafficking and exposing children to sexual abuse and begging as shown in the article by Sasha Poucki and Nicole Bryan. Also included in this special issue is an article that addresses the question of the health of trafficked women that are exposed to violence, abuse, and risk. The article by Arun Kumar refers to physical, mental, and sexual health of women and girls of Mexico City, but it is indicative of a prevailing precarious situation for all trafficked people worldwide.

Women and girls are victimized all over the world and are disproportionately the victims of human trafficking, particularly for sexual exploitation or offers of false marriage proposals. While structural poverty caused by globalization is a large contributing push factor, there are many other complex factors at play that add to the vulnerability of women to be trafficked. Gender inequality and the feminization of poverty are also large contributing factors. Patriarchal societies that reinforce the subjugation of women and deeply entrenched sociocultural norms leave women and girls disproportionately more vulnerable to fall victim to traffickers. Ethnicity and race, as markers of oppression and subordination, combined with internal patriarchal values, have played a role in the trafficking of persons as shown in the cases of Nepal, an arguing point highlighted by Shoba Gurung, and Mexico with indigenous Raramuri girls trafficked by deception. Strict cultural norms, customs, and traditions also discriminate against women further. These norms are particularly prevalent in South Asia where young women and girls are often seen as nothing more than commodities and sold into marriage for high dowries at young ages. When families face hardship and struggle to survive, girls are the ones usually targeted to help out and are often pulled out of schools and forced to work at young ages to support their families. It is the view and practice in some societies that girls and young women can be sold to pay debt bondage.

In her contribution, Shobha Gurung observes that trafficking and the sex trade industry have expanded and intensified in South Asia posing a number of structural questions related to the development of transnational capitalism, but also, to the implications of patriarchal culture, gender discrimination, and inter-ethnic relations. Precisely, because trafficking is related to multiple factors, the theoretical intersectional approach suggested by feminist research is indeed helpful. In all the articles of this issue, a number of structural and systemic factors collude with cultural and subjective practices in a complex context of cultural and gendered oppression.

To close the approach of intersectionality and to highlight the role of cultural patterns as a leading path for research on trafficking, the final article by Natividad Gutierrez Chong, questions whether race and ethnicity account for the global trafficking of women and girls; and if the sex industry has established stereotyped patterns of Mexican male consumption. She also gathers other examples from Latin America, Europe and Asia to illustrate her point.

As this special issue addresses culture and trafficking in a globalized word, we would like to say some final words on the research methods used. Trafficked people thrown into prostitution, forced marriages, or begging are hidden and as such remain a challenge for the researcher. Already classical methods such as snowball sampling and direct observation of genderised places – i.e., carpet factories, bars, massage parlors, 'red light' streets, and so on – would remain a helpful ground for further ethnographic enquiry. Interviews and focus groups when possible remain also a prime source of data. And, as we all know the study of trafficking does not rely on statistics or official first-hand data, there is always room for the work of imagination and assumption. Since the trafficked population remains hidden, and the activity is linked to organized crime and carried out under the blind eye of complicity and a net of corruption, other research strategies have to be put in motion. Take the case of cultural artifacts of mass entertainment contrived for male consumption such as video games, film industry, and popular literature. The stereotyped sexual preferences of urban male consumers of Mexico City were found in the reading material of popular literature and its advertising pages.

Concluding Remarks

Eradicating human trafficking requires a multipronged approach. The study of human trafficking is multidisciplinary. It encompasses sociology, psychology, anthropology, criminal justice, economics, and political science, to name a few. There is a pressing need for effective cooperation and coordination of research, a forum where research results can be exchanged between academics, researchers, and other entities such as supranational bodies and governments.

The articles in this special issue hope to shed some light on the scope, nature, and reality of human trafficking. The academic contributors to this edition are multidisciplinary and come from different countries. The articles situate human trafficking within the global context and at the same time focus on particular aspects of the manifestation and consequences of trafficking regionally. Human trafficking is an indisputable reality. The authors in this special edition hope that by working together one day human trafficking will no longer exist.

The Forces Driving Global Migration

Stephen Castles

Movements of people are a crucial element in global integration. Most destination countries favour entry of the highly skilled, but restrict entry of lower-skilled workers, asylum seekers and refugees. A major cause of migration is the growing inequality in incomes and human security between more- and less-developed countries. Further driving factors include uneven economic development; rapid demographic transitions; and technological advances in transport and communications. Increasingly migrants do not shift their social existence from one society to another, but maintain transnational connections. The global economic crisis since 2008 has brought a hiatus in some of these factors, but has not undermined their long-term significance. Australia's traditional model of permanent-settlement migration needs to be adjusted to the new realities of global mobility and connectivity.

Global Migration Trends

UN Department of Economic and Social Affairs (UNDESA) data indicate that there were some 214 million international migrants worldwide in 2010. This compares with just 156 million migrants in 1990. However, since global population has grown at the same time, the share of migrants in the world population has not changed much increasing from 2.9 per cent in 1990 to 3.1 per cent in 2010 (see Appendix Table 1).

What makes international migration highly significant in economic and political terms is its concentration: certain locations have become major emigration areas (such as the Philippines, Indonesia and Sri Lanka), while other locations have become major poles of attraction, such as South Korea, Malaysia, Singapore – and of course Australia, which, with 27 per cent (at the 2011 Census), has the highest overseas-born share in its population of any immigration country (apart from the special cases of Israel and the states of the Arab Gulf).

The UNDESA figures (see Appendix Figures 1 and 2) show that migrants are highly concentrated in the more-developed countries (MDCs) and much less so in less-developed countries (LDCs). In 1990, 53 per cent of international migrants were to be found in the MDCs, which, however, were only home to 22 per cent of the world's people. By 2010, 60 per cent of migrants were estimated to be in MDCs, which then accounted for only 18 per cent of the world's people. To put it differently, 10 out of every 100 persons in MDCs were immigrants in 2010, compared with 1.5 per 100 in LDCs. With regard to refugees, the picture was very different (see Appendix Table 1 and Figure 3). Global refugee numbers declined from about 18 million in 1990 to under 14 million in 2005, only to increase to over 16 million in 2010. Today, over 85 per cent of the world's refugees are concentrated in LDCs, and only 14 per cent in the richer MDCs.

For many years now, the UN Population Division (which is part of UNDESA) has been arguing that international migration is growing only slightly faster than world population, but that migration from LDCs to MDCs is growing much more rapidly. Neo-liberal globalisation since the late 1970s has been linked to a significant increase in international migration. This is often regarded as South–North migration, but the South–North breakdown is too crude to capture the very significant economic growth that is taking place in many areas that were once considered part of the Global South. Indeed, migration within the Asian region is very much the result of uneven processes of economic development, with migrant workers moving from countries with strong demographic growth but slower economic growth, to emerging industrial economies, which are often already experiencing a rapid demographic transition. However, a great deal of migration is not primarily economically motivated: forced migration remains widespread, and people also migrate for purposes of family reunion, marriage, education and lifestyle.

In addition, focusing just on international migration can give a deceptive picture. Many people move within their own countries. Internal migration attracts less political attention, but its volume in population giants like China, India, Indonesia, Brazil and Nigeria is far greater than that of international movements, and the social and cultural consequences can be equally important. In China, the 'floating population' of people moving from the central and western provinces to the new industrial areas of the east coast numbers at least 100 million, and many of them experience legal disadvantage and economic marginalisation very much like international migrants elsewhere (Skeldon 2006). It is impossible to know the exact numbers of internal migrants, although the UN Development Program estimated some 740 million in 2009 (UNDP 2009).

Drivers of International Migration

Global economic integration is an important factor encouraging international migration, but a purely economic understanding of migration can be misleading. This article, therefore, reviews a range of drivers or causal factors and examines the linkages between them. 'Drivers' refers not only to factors that encourage cross-border mobility, but also to factors that help shape the forms taken by movements. The term does not imply determinism: except in the case of emergency migration to escape violence or disaster, there is always an element of choice or agency in the decision to migrate – after all, the majority of people chose not to do so. I see 'drivers' as factors that increase the likelihood that people will decide to leave their homes in search of a better life. The following factors will be discussed here: neo-liberal globalisation and social transformation; inequality; state security and human security; technology; labour demand; demographic changes; politics; law and governance; the social dynamics of migration; and the role of people who make their living by facilitating migration (sometimes called 'the migration industry').

Since each factor is highly complex and linked in manifold ways to the others, my treatment here will inevitably be rather brief and superficial. The article will conclude with some speculations on possible future perspectives in international migration. The article does not address internal migration, but that does not imply that it is in any way less important than international movements.

Neo-liberal Globalisation and Social Transformation

The industrial revolution that took place in Britain in the 18th and 19th centuries was linked to an agricultural revolution resulting from the growth of commercial farming and the enclosure of arable land for pasture. The shift from traditional to commercial farming was in itself partly a result of the re-investment of superprofits made in the colonies through plantation agriculture based on slavery. The displaced tenant farmers moved to emerging industrial towns where they were available as workers for the new factories. They were soon joined by destitute artisans, such as hand-loom weavers, who had lost their livelihood through competition from the new manufacturers. This 'primitive accumulation' as Karl Marx called it (1976, pp. 873–876) lay the basis of the new 'free' working class which was crucial for industrialisation.

Today, one can observe similar processes taking place on a global scale. As LDCs in Africa, Asia and Latin America are drawn into global economic linkages, powerful processes of social transformation are unleashed. Neo-liberal forms of international economic integration undermine traditional ways of working and living (Stiglitz 2002). The 'Green Revolution' (i.e. increased agricultural productivity based on use of chemicals, irrigation and machinery) displaces people from the land. Displaced farmers migrate into burgeoning cities like Sao Paolo, Shanghai, Calcutta or Jakarta.

It is estimated that 95 per cent of future population growth will take place in the urban areas of LDCs, about half of it in slum areas, leading to forecasts of some '2 billion slum-dwellers by 2030 or 2040' (Davis 2006, p. 151). In future, climate change may exacerbate the situation: possible declines in rural productivity due to drought or extreme weather events may encourage mobility, but the destination areas – often poor areas of low-lying cities on coasts or river-deltas – are frequently themselves highly vulnerable to changes caused by global climate change (Foresight 2011, Piguet *et al.* 2011).

The move to the cities is driven not only by loss of rural livelihoods, but by the hope of better opportunities and higher incomes in urban settings. Many rural–urban migrants do in fact benefit – at least in the long run – by getting better jobs, becoming entrepreneurs or securing improved education and health services (Saunders 2011). Others find themselves caught in a cycle of unemployment and insecure informal sector work. There are few formal sector jobs for the millions of newcomers. Standards of housing, health and education are poor, while crime, violence and human rights violations are rife. Such conditions are powerful motivations to seek better livelihoods elsewhere, either in growth areas within the region or in the Global North.

Indeed, it is often people with more resources – whether financial or educational – who are able to move internationally and particularly over long distances. Migrants often come from middle-income backgrounds. Typically, the most impoverished people in less-developed cannot migrate internationally, because they cannot afford the costs of mobility. The migration of middle-income people is driven partly by the hope of better livelihoods elsewhere, but also by lack of opportunities at home. The structural adjustment programmes imposed on many southern countries by the International Monetary Fund (IMF) and World Bank have extended the crisis to middle-class occupations, by forcing states to drastically cut education, health and welfare. This has caused many administrators and professionals to migrate – conveniently providing highly skilled personnel for the North (see Adepoju 2000).

At the same time, globalisation leads to social transformation in the North. In the rich member countries of the Organisation for Economic Cooperation and Development (OECD), industrial restructuring since the late 1970s has meant deskilling and early retirement for many workers. The new services industries need very different types of labour. But, due to declining fertility, smaller cohorts of young nationals are entering the labour market than in the past. As educational opportunities improve, few young nationals are willing to do low-skilled work. Developed countries have high demand for both high- and low-skilled workers and need migrants – whether regular or irregular.

This complementarity between processes of social transformation in LDCs and MDCs is a powerful driver of international migration (Castles 2010). Both public and policy discourses have tended to focus on the economic side of South–North differences. This is indeed important, but it is far from the only factor involved. People rarely leave their home communities just to gain higher incomes, as long as their ways of living and working are still viable. It is the undermining of these modes of existence that triggers departure.

A critique of 19th century liberal economic theories based on the idea of an economy 'disembedded' from society and efficiently regulated by the profit principle alone was provided by Karl Polanyi in his book on the 'great transformation' (Polanyi 2001). Today these theories have been revived in the form of neo-liberalism (Hayek 1991), providing an ideological justification for a process of globalisation based ostensibly on free market forces alone (Munck 2009). Even in triumphal periods of global capitalism, such as that following the collapse of the Soviet Union, this ideology has caused massive damage (Stiglitz 2002). This applies even more strongly today, in the context of the global economic crisis (Phillips 2011b).

Inequality

A crucial claim made by advocates of neo-liberal globalisation in its boom years from the mid-1970s to 2007 was that that it would lead to faster economic growth in poor countries, and thus, in the long run, to poverty reduction and convergence with richer countries. In fact, the opposite was the case: according to a senior World Bank economist, global inequality by the mid-2000s was 'probably the highest ever recorded' (Milanovic 2007, p. 39). Rates of absolute poverty have been reduced in some places – particularly in China, South Korea and Vietnam, although sometimes inequality has increased at the same time. Yet the claim of reducing inequality was a main element of political legitimation, because it underpinned the principles of 'open borders' and 'a level playing field'. Flows across borders – of commodities, capital, technology and labour – were meant to secure optimal allocation of resources and to ensure that production factors could be obtained at the lowest possible cost.

Liberalisation of flows was never complete – for instance rich countries protected their own agriculture while demanding the removal of barriers for others. But the hypocrisy was greatest with regard to flows of people, where control of movements across borders was often seen as an important part of nation-state sovereignty. Economists argued that the removal of restrictions on human mobility would lead to large increases in global income and would help reduce North–South inequality (Borjas 1989, Straubhaar and Zimmermann 1992). Politicians in labour-importing countries, however, were aware of popular suspicion of immigration, and responded with a rhetoric of national interests and control (see below). Governments around the world try to resolve the contradiction between strong labour demand and public hostility to migration by creating entry systems that encourage legal entry of highly skilled workers, while either excluding lower-skilled workers or regulating them through temporary employment schemes. Since labour market demand for the lower-skilled is strong, millions of migrants are pushed into irregularity (Castles *et al.* 2013). Governments often turn a blind eye to this in times of economic growth, and then tighten up border security and deport irregulars in times of recession.

National migration rules differentiate people on the basis of origins, gender, human capital and legal status. International migration is thus more a result of inequality than a tool to alleviate it. The differences in income levels delineated by North–South borders (most dramatically perhaps that between the US and Mexico) are indeed enormous, but opportunities of crossing those borders are far from equal.

State Security and Human Security

Since the beginning of the 21st century, governments have increasingly portrayed migration as a threat to security. The terrorist attacks in New York on 11 September 2001, the 2004 bombings in Madrid and the 2005 bombings in London led to a widespread belief that Muslim migrants can constitute a danger to democratic societies. This ignores the fact that the overwhelming majority of Muslims oppose fundamentalism and that very few of those involved in these attacks were either migrants or refugees. The idea of immigrants – and particularly those of Muslim background – as a potential 'enemy within' is not new (Guild 2009). Indeed immigrants have for centuries been seen as a threat to state security and national identity. Before Muslims, a succession of other groups was cast in this role (Cohen 1994). Such attitudes have in turn been used to justify immigration restrictions and reductions in civil liberties – often not just for immigrants but for the population as a whole.

The securitisation of migration and ethnic minorities is based on a perspective that emphasises the security of rich northern states and their populations, while ignoring the reality that migration and refugee flows are often the result of the fundamental lack of human security in many poorer countries. Such insecurity – which finds its expression in poverty, hunger, violence and lack of human rights – is not in any way a natural condition, but is a result of past practices of colonisation and more recent economic and political power structures, which have exacerbated inequality in many places. Migration policies too can exacerbate human insecurity. Where states refuse to create legal migration systems despite strong employer demand for workers, migrants experience high levels of risk and exploitation. Smuggling, trafficking, bonded labour and lack of human and worker rights are the fate of millions of migrants.

Technology

The technical advances associated with globalisation encourage mobility. Here it is difficult to distinguish between the effects of new technologies and shifts in culture – indeed one can see technology itself as an expression of culture. Electronic communications provide knowledge of migration routes and work opportunities, thus serving as a material basis for the development of 'cultural capital'. Migrants are often pioneers in the use of new communication techniques, starting with use of audio cassettes and then video to keep in touch with families and homeland culture in the 1960s and 1970s, and going on to email, social media and mobile phones today.

Similarly, long-distance travel has become cheaper and more accessible, and this can help to strengthen migrant 'social capital'; once migratory flows are established they generate 'migration networks'; previous migrants help members of their families or communities with information on work, accommodation and official rules. Such networks are not new, but become more effective and durable in a situation of easy communications and travel. Increasingly, migrant networks form the basis for transnational communities – groups of people who have significant political, economic, social and cultural links that go across national borders (Portes *et al.* 1999). The relative ease of long-distance travel also helps explain the growth of ethnic diversity in destination countries. Back in the 1960s, most Western European countries recruited migrants from a quite small range of origin countries; today migrants come from much further afield and exhibit a bewildering variety of cultural and religious backgrounds.

Labour Demand

It is often argued that labour migration from poor to rich countries meets mutual needs. LDCs have too many young labour market entrants for their weak economies to employ, so they 'need' to export surplus workers. MDCs and emerging industrial economies, by contrast, have declining numbers of young people entering their labour markets and cannot fill the growing numbers of jobs, so they 'need' to import labour. But it is important to realise that the 'need' to export labour from the South is a result of historical processes of colonisation and expropriation of resources, while the 'need' for low-skilled labour in northern countries is socially constructed by the poor wages, conditions and social status in certain sectors (Münz *et al.* 2007, p. 7). If the conditions and status of such jobs were improved, local workers might be more willing to take them while marginal employers might go out of business. The result might be that certain types of work would become unviable, and be relocated in lower-wage economies in the South.

Such 'off-shoring' or 'outsourcing' has in fact been common since the 1970s in the manufacturing sector, where much of the production has been moved to new industrial economies. Agriculture also seems an obvious choice for outsourcing, since productivity is low. However, local agribusiness would be hurt by moving production off-shore, and has had the political clout to prevent this happening. This explains the persistence of the EU's Common Agricultural Policy and US farm subsidies, both of which are costly to tax payers, disadvantageous to consumers and damaging to agriculture in poor countries (Oxfam 2002). More recently, a trend has emerged for the outsourcing of 'back office' operations such as bank call centres, and even of some design and development work, to make use of reserves of qualified white-collar workers in such countries as India and the Philippines.

Rather than a *need* for migrant labour, we should therefore be analysing a *demand* promoted by powerful economic and political interests. Government policies in receiving countries have responded either by creating recruitment and management systems for legal foreign labour, or by tacitly permitting (and sometimes regularising) irregular employment of migrants.

Foreign labour employment in Europe stagnated or declined after 1973 in a period of recession and restructuring, just as Australian immigration declined at this time. Many European countries adopted 'zero immigration policies', but were unable to prevent family reunion and permanent settlement. The US Government changed its immigration rules in 1965 to remove restrictions on non-Europeans, but did not expect a significant increase in entries from non-traditional sources. However, the early 1990s saw an upsurge of migration to developed countries, driven by both economic and political factors. The reaction of policy-makers was to tighten up national immigration restrictions and to increase international cooperation on border control.

In recent years there has been a gradual shift in official views. A major factor was the realisation that developed countries could not export all low-skilled work to low-wage countries. Manufacturing could be shifted to China, Brazil or Malaysia, but the construction industry, catering and hospitals had to be where their customers lived. From 1995 to 2005 there was sustained growth in OECD economies (the advanced industrial countries of Europe, North America, Oceania, Japan and Korea), leading to strong demand for labour. By 2005, foreign-born workers made up 25 per cent of the labour force in Australia and Switzerland, 20 per cent in Canada, 15 per cent in the US, New Zealand, Austria and Germany, and around 12 per cent in other Western European countries. Migrants made up between one-third and two-thirds of new employees in most Western and Southern European countries from 1995 to 2005 (OECD 2007, pp. 63–66).

Immigrants are vital not only because they fill jobs, but also because they bring skills with them. The old stereotype of the unskilled migrant coming in to take the least-qualified positions is no longer valid. In Belgium, Luxemburg, Sweden and Denmark, over 40 per cent of the employed migrants who arrived from 1995 to 2005 had tertiary education. In France the figure was 35 per cent and in the Netherlands 30 per cent. In many cases, migrant worker had higher qualification profiles than local-born workers (OECD 2007, pp. 67–68).

Demographic Change

One reason for the shift in approaches by destination-country governments was a realisation of the extent of demographic change. Eurostat projections showed that the population of the European Union (in this case the EU25, i.e. the EU countries after the 2004 enlargement) was likely to fall by 1.5 per cent from 457 million in 2004 to 450 million by 2050. However, the decline was forecast to be much greater in Germany (9.6 per cent), Italy (8.9 per cent) and the 10 mainly Eastern and Central European 'Accession States', which joined the EU in 2004 (11.7 per cent). More serious still was the decline in working age population (15–64); in 2005 in the EU25, 67 per cent of the population were of working age, compared with 16 per cent of 65 and over. By 2050, a working age population of 57 per cent would have to support 30 per cent aged 65 and over (CEC 2005; see Appendix Tables 1 and 2). As the European Commission (EC) argued (CEC 2005, § 1.2):

> In the short to mid-term, labour immigration can [. . .] positively contribute to tackling the effects of this demographic evolution and will prove crucial to satisfying current and future labour market needs and thus ensure economic sustainability and growth.

Demographic trends are less alarming in the US – partly as a result of the effects of past migration on the age structure and fertility. Australia shares this situation, but even here, the writing is on the wall; the ageing of the population and the decline in the share of working age people is already being forecast (Swan 2010). Other industrial areas – most notably Japan and S. Korea – already share the demographic dilemma of Europe.

An important social factor is closely linked to the demographic shifts. The proportion of children aged 0–14 in the EU25 population was projected to fall from 16.4 per cent in 2004 to 13.4 per cent in 2050 (CEC 2005; see Appendix Table 2). If there are fewer young people, they will expect better educational opportunities, and few of them will accept low-skilled jobs. European experts now forecast that manual jobs in manufacturing and agriculture may decline, but there is likely to be a growth in unmet demand for low-skilled service workers in household and care jobs (Münz *et al.* 2007, p. 9).

Yet northern policy-makers seems to believe that the less-developed areas of Asia, Latin America and Africa can provide unlimited reserves of labour with the necessary skills and attributes to meet labour-market demand for the foreseeable future. This belief in an endless supply of willing migrants is short-sighted for two reasons. First, demographic transitions from pre-industrial high fertility and high mortality patterns to lower mortality and fertility are taking place even in the poorest regions, so that global labour reserves may be much lower by 2050 (UNDP 2009). Already developed countries are competing to attract highly skilled workers through privileged entry rules. As demographic gaps and economic demand for workers increases, even lower-skilled workers may become scarce. For instance, rapid economic growth in China is beginning to create structural labour shortages (Pieke 2011).

Politics

Politics is crucial in determining the forms taken by international migration: especially by differentiating between 'wanted' groups (especially highly skilled personnel and their families), who can cross borders and take up work in safety and with a fair measure of legal protection, and 'unwanted' categories (especially lower-skilled workers and asylum seekers), who face high levels of risk and exploitation.

International migration has become a key area of national politics, particularly in destination countries. In the early years of foreign labour recruitment – for instance in Western Europe in the 1960s – employers and politicians could build a national consensus around the benefits of employing 'guestworkers', but as concerns about new migratory currents and increased population diversity developed, especially from the 1990s onwards, migration policy became increasingly politicised and polarised. The effects of economic restructuring on jobs and social relations were blamed on migrants, as visible symbols of globalisation and loss of national identity (Vasta and Castles 1996). Politicians across the political spectrum tried to outbid each other in anti-immigration rhetoric.

Yet at the same time, policy-makers knew that important sectors of the economy would only remain viable if they could import labour. Moreover, the very conservative politicians who fulminated about threats to national identity were often highly sensitive to the wishes of industrial and agricultural employers. Policy approaches to international migration are therefore full of contradictions (Castles 2004, 2007). A central contradiction is that between state and market: policy-makers seek to admit only those migrants seen by the public as economically productive and politically acceptable, while employers demand workers of all types and skill levels. Often migration rules signal migrants to stay out, while the market signals that they are welcome.

In any case, official rules are often hypocritical: governments use 'crack-downs' on irregular migrants as a way of appeasing public opinion, while tacitly permitting irregular labour migration to meet employer demand – the USA has led the way on this (Passel and Cohn 2009), but Italy (Reyneri 2001), Spain, Malaysia, Japan, the UK and many other states have similar practices (Düvell 2006a). Many employers actually prefer irregular migrants, because they lack rights, cannot complain to authorities or trade unions and are therefore easily exploitable.

The stated objective of government policy is often strict immigration control, but governments also want to support national industries and help them to obtain the labour they seek. Thus publicly announced objectives and actual policy do not always match up. However, the interplay between the market forces demanding freedom of movement and the political forces demanding control can be seen as highly effective in creating a global labour market stratified not only according to 'human capital' (possession of education, training and work skills), but also according to gender, race, ethnicity, origins and legal status (Castles 2011b). The new global labour market is an expression of a global class hierarchy, in which people with high human capital from rich countries have almost unlimited rights of mobility, while others are differentiated, controlled and included or excluded in a variety of ways (Bauman 1998).

Law and Governance

In a world of freedom of human movements – a demand both of liberal economists (Nayar 1994, Straubhaar 2002, Bhagwati 2003) and human rights advocates (Hayter

2001, Harris 2002, Pécoud and de Guchteneire 2007) – there could by definition be no irregular migration. *Open borders* would be the simplest way of eliminating irregular migration, but political considerations hinder governments from adopting this.

Irregular migration can be seen as the result of state laws and regulations, which label certain forms of mobility as legal and desirable, and others as illegal and unwanted (Castles *et al.* 2013). The strong emphasis on people-smuggling and trafficking by politicians and international agencies legitimates stricter control and greater selectivity. It makes it possible to limit the human rights of 'unwanted' migrants, which in turn makes it easier to exploit them. Some observers emphasise the state's right to control entry to the territory as an enduring aspect of national sovereignty. However, an historical survey by Düvell (2006b, pp. 21–29) reveals very little use of the concept of illegal migration before World War II. Essentially, it became widespread after the abandonment of migrant labour recruitment schemes by European nations in the mid-1970s.

On the other hand, states show a marked reluctance to accept international legal norms designed to protect the rights of migrants. Globalisation has led to the establishment of institutions of global governance, such as the IMF and the World Bank for finance and the World Trade Organisation (WTO) for trade. Migration, by contrast, has been seen as a preserve of national sovereignty. There is a serious governance deficit; the international community has failed to build institutions to ensure orderly migration, protect the human rights of migrants and maximise development benefits (Bhagwati 2003). Elements of an international framework do exist in International Labour Organisation (ILO) Conventions No. 97 of 1949 and No. 143 of 1975, and in the 1990 United Nations Convention on the Protection of the Rights of All Migrant Workers and Members of Their Families. Yet the latter had only been ratified by 44 nations in 2010 – out of the 193 members of the UN! Emigration countries have been concerned with reducing internal labour surpluses and maximising remittances. Immigration countries have been reluctant to take steps which might increase labour costs.

Some regional bodies seek to cooperate on migration. The EU has gone furthest by introducing free movement for citizens of member states, and common policies towards asylum and migration from non-members. In 2003, A Global Commission on International Migration convened by the UN Secretary General took up its work. The GCIM Report (GCIM 2005) argued that migration should 'become an integral part of national, regional and global strategies for economic growth, in both the developing and the developed world'. The GCIM put forward proposals for maximising the benefits of international migration, including measures to limit the 'brain drain', to prevent smuggling and trafficking, to encourage the flow of remittances and to enhance the role of diasporas as agents of development.

Migration and development was the topic of a High Level Dialogue (HLD) of ministers and senior officials at the UN General Assembly in September 2006. This led to the establishment of a Global Forum on Migration and Development (GMFD), which met annually from 2007 to 2012. A second HLD is planned for 2013. The

GMFD and HLD have no decision-making powers; they fulfil a merely advisory role, and powerful states have been unwilling to implement any measures that might lead to higher costs for migrant labour. However, migrant associations and civil society organisations have seen these bodies as useful venues for demanding new approaches to migration based on the human rights of migrants and their families (Castles 2011a).

The Social Dynamics of Migration

All too often both government policies and public perceptions are based on the idea of migrants as economic beings, whose motivations are determined by narrow cost–benefit considerations. They ignore the social relationships of migrants as members of families and communities, as well as the way personal characteristics and goals change over the human life cycle. Anthropologists and sociologists use the concept of *migrant agency* to analyse the ways in which migrants actively shape migratory processes to achieve better outcomes for themselves, their families and their communities. Migration is a social process, in which the participants undergo processes of change, and in turn act to change the conditions and practices that they encounter. These social dynamics play an important role in shaping the volume and forms of international migration.

Migration decisions are often made not by individuals, but by families. In situations of rapid change, a family may decide to send one or more members to work in another region or country, in order to maximise income and survival chances. Remittances sent home by irregular migrants can help lift families out of poverty and may contribute to investments and economic development. Family linkages often provide both the financial and the cultural capital (that is the knowledge of opportunities and means of mobility), which make migration possible.

Motivations change over the migrants' life cycle: in economic migration, the primary migrant is usually a young man or women in search of temporary work, who often intends to return home once certain savings targets have been reached. Difficulty in achieving such targets may lead to prolonged stay. This in turn encourages family reunion or formation. People start to see their life perspectives in the new country. Once migrants' children go to school in the new country, learn the language, join peer groups and develop bicultural or transcultural identities, it becomes very difficult for the parents to leave.

Migration laws and rules often ignore the social nature of the migratory process, and fragment communities into individuals who are meant to fit into specific bureaucratic categories. Such categories may not correspond to economic and social realities, and the result may be irregular migration and residence. People lucky enough to enjoy a middle-class position in developed countries tend to have a positive view of the state and the law. The majority of the world's population, who live in inefficient, corrupt and sometimes violent states, may see things differently.

They have to cope despite the state, not because of it. From this perspective, migration rules become just another barrier to be overcome in order to survive.

Migrant agency is important within destination countries too. Experiences of exploitation and insecurity may lead to resistance. Recent years have witnessed an upsurge in protest movements of disadvantaged and vulnerable groups such as migrant women, irregular workers, ethnic and racial minorities. In 2005 for example, youth of mainly North African origin rioted in protest against social exclusion and police brutality in many urban periphery regions all around France. In 2006, migrant construction workers in Dubai, many of them working on the world's highest building, the Burj Dubai (since renamed the Burj Khalifa), went on strike. Also in 2006, migrants in the USA protested against proposed laws, which would have criminalised irregular migrants. On 10 April, millions of people demonstrated in 102 cities, with the largest single gathering of around half a million in Los Angeles. Then, in late 2007, migrant-origin youth in France took to the streets again in protest against the deaths of two youths, electrocuted while trying to escape from the police.

Such movements present challenges to both the economic principles of neo-liberal globalisation and to the social exclusion experienced in labour-importing states. Their spontaneity and lack of conventional leadership make it hard to fit them into conventional frameworks. Resistance to the structural inequality in incomes and human security inherent in the global labour market makes it clear that migrants are not passive victims, but are capable of developing new forms of political and social actions.

The 'Migration Industry'

As so often in contemporary life, if the rules imposed by governments and bureaucracies become too complex, it may be necessary to seek professional help. Another driver of migration is thus the fast-growing business sector of people who help facilitate migration. This so-called 'migration industry' includes migration agents, travel bureaus, bankers, lawyer, labour recruiters, interpreters and housing brokers. Migration agents sometimes include members of a migrant community such as shopkeepers, priests, teachers and other community leaders, who help their compatriots on a voluntary or part-time basis. Facilitating migration is a major and mainly legal international business (Salt and Clarke 2000, p. 327). For example, most recruitment of migrant workers for Gulf oil states and emerging East and Southeast Asian economies is organised by migration agents and labour brokers.

While some agents carry out legitimate activities, others deceive and exploit workers. There is sometimes no clear division between organisations providing legitimate recruitment and travel services, and those indulging in people smuggling or trafficking. The migration industry consists of people who make their living by facilitating migration. They are likely to go on doing so, even if government policies change. The form of migration may change – for instance from legal worker recruitment to asylum migration or undocumented entry – but the volume may be undiminished. Thus the more governments try to control borders the greater the flows of undocumented migrants seem to be. Governments remain focused on national control models, while migrants follow the transnational logic of globalised labour markets.

Future Perspectives

It would be foolish to make predictions about likely future trends in migration. Before thinking ahead – say to 2050 – we should look back by the same margin and consider whether the current migratory situation could have been predicted in 1970. No observer then imagined the massive expansion, globalisation and politicisation of migration that has in fact taken place. However, it is interesting to think through current trends, and to speculate on unexpected events that can lead to major shifts.

One such event was the 'Oil Crisis' that started in 1973, and proved to be the harbinger of major changes: large corporations shifted their investment strategies away from manufacturing in the old core industrial areas, and developed off-shore production areas in low-wage economies. This led to a loss of blue-collar jobs and a decline of labour migration to Western Europe, but instead of leaving as expected, many foreign workers stayed on, brought in their families and became permanent settlers. At the same time, new patterns of labour migration to the oil-rich states and to the new industrial areas (especially in Asia) emerged.

This leads to the question: could the multi-stage global economic crisis since 2007 similarly lead to major shifts in migratory patterns? Initially, the effects of the down-turn in North America and Europe on migration and remittances were less than predicted by many analysts in late 2008. However, by 2010, the enduring economic stagnation had led to falls in migration, especially of low-skilled irregular workers. For instance, Mexican migration to the USA had dropped sharply (Passel and Cohn 2011). But it is not yet clear whether the economic crisis will alter the fundamental forces that bring about international flows of people in an increasingly inter-linked world (Phillips 2011a). Economic inequality and the demographic imbalances between the ageing populations of the North and the large cohorts of working-age persons in the South remain important factors in generating migration. At the same time, the improvements in transport and communications inherent in globalisation make it easier for people to live their lives in expanded social and cultural spaces, which have little to do with the borders of nation-states. Old nationalist ideas of homogeneous national populations, whose political, economic, social and cultural horizons are contained within state borders, seem increasingly unrealistic.

Yet, states still have the power to differentiate between those who can be mobile under conditions of safety and dignity (especially the privileged and highly skilled), and those who are forced to risk injury and exploitation in order to seek better livelihoods elsewhere (mainly lower-skilled workers and asylum seekers). In the long run this unequal migration order may not prove sustainable. At present, policy-makers in highly developed countries seem to believe that there is an inexhaustible supply of labour available in LDCs. This may be so for the next few decades, but it is unlikely to be so for much longer. The demographic transition to lower mortality and fertility is taking place everywhere. By the middle of this century, many areas in Latin America, South and Southeast Asia and Africa may begin to experience their own labour shortages. They may no longer have reserves of young labour-market entrants, willing to accept high levels of risk and exploitation in order to migrate as low-skilled workers to today's highly developed economies.

The demographic and economic demand factors for migrants are likely to remain strong in the North, but states may have to work towards a new migration order based not on a one-sided power monopoly, but on cooperation between origin and destination states and all the social groups affected. It will become crucial to reconceptualise migration not as a problem to be solved through strict control, but as a normal part of global change and development, in which decision-makers should aim to minimise potential negative effects and to help realise the potential benefits for the migrants as well as for the economies and the societies involved.

An important step towards fairer and more effective migration policies is a fundamental change in attitudes. It is important to see migration not as threat to state security, but as a result of the human insecurity that arises through global inequality. Throughout human history, people have migrated in order to improve their livelihoods and to gain greater security. Migration is an important aspect of human development. This idea corresponds with Amartya Sen's principle of 'development as freedom' (Sen 2001). According to this, mobility is a basic freedom, and has the potential to lead to greater human capabilities. Reducing migration restrictions and ensuring that people can move safely and legally helps enhance human rights, and also can lead to greater economic efficiency and social equality (UNDP 2009). This human development approach could provide a new frame of reference for thinking about migration and diversity. Fairer national policies and global governance of migration should be an integral part of comprehensive development strategies designed to reduce global inequality.

Australian policy-makers – like those of other developed countries – still focus on the perceived economic benefits of migration. This is used to justify the preference for highly skilled migrants that frequently contradicts the interests of origin countries. The recent growth in temporary migration – both of workers and of students – is also based on short-term economic interests. Australian public discourse largely ignores the social and cultural factors that are reshaping migratory flows. When it comes to the inequality and human insecurity that help drive migration, Australian policies and attitudes still tend to be inward-looking and exclusionary. It is to be hoped that better understanding of the complex factors behind contemporary human mobility will help Australia move towards more sustainable and balanced approaches.

Acknowledgements

The author thanks two anonymous referees for their detailed and helpful comments.

References

Adepoju, A., 2000. Issues and recent trends in international migration in sub-Saharan Africa. *International social science journal*, 165, 383–394.

Bauman, Z., 1998. *Globalization: the human consequences*. Cambridge: Polity.

Bhagwati, J., 2003. Borders beyond control. *Foreign affairs*, 82 (1), 98–104.

Borjas, G.J., 1989. Economic theory and international migration. *International migration review*, 23 (3), 457–485.

Castles, S., 2004. Why migration policies fail. *Ethnic and racial studies*, 27 (2), 205–227.

Castles, S., 2007. The factors that make and unmake migration policies. *In*: A. Portes and J. DeWind, eds. *Rethinking migration: new theoretical and empirical perspectives*. New York and Oxford: Berghahn, 29–61.

Castles, S., 2010. Understanding global migration: a social transformation perspective. *Journal of ethnic and migration studies*, 36 (10), 1565–1586.

Castles, S., 2011a. Bringing human rights into the migration and development debate. *Global policy*, 2 (3), 248–258.

Castles, S., 2011b. Migration, crisis and the global labour market. *Globalizations*, 8 (3), 311–324.

Castles, S., Arias Cubas, M., Kim, C. and Ozkul, D., 2013. Irregular migration: causes, patterns and strategies. *In*: I. Omelaniuk and National Institute for Migration Mexico (INAMI), eds. *Reflections on migration and development*. Berlin and Geneva: Springer and International Organization for Migration.

Commission of the European Communities [CEC], 2005. *Communication from the commission: policy plan on legal migration*, COM (2005)669 final. Brussels: Commission of the European Communities.

Cohen, R., 1994. *Frontiers of identity: the British and the others*. London: Longman.

Davis, M., 2006. *Planet of slums*. London and New York: Verso.

Düvell, F. ed., 2006a. *Illegal immigration in Europe: beyond control*. Basingstoke: Palgrave/Macmillan.

Düvell, F., 2006b. Introduction and background. *In*: F. Düvell, ed. *Illegal immigration in Europe: beyond control?* Basingstoke: Palgrave Macmillan, 3–39.

Foresight, 2011. *Foresight: migration and global environmental change*. London: UK Government Office for Science. Available from: http://www.bis.gov.uk/assets/foresight/docs/migration/11-1116-migration-and-global-environmental-change.pdf. [Accessed 22 March 2012].

Global Commission on International Migration [GCIM], 2005. *Migration in an interconnected world: new directions for action: report of the global commission on international migration*. Geneva: Global Commission on International Migration. Available from: http://www.gcim.org/en/finalreport.html [Accessed 1 June 2006].

Guild, E., 2009. *Security and migration in the 21st century*. Cambridge: Polity.

Harris, N., 2002. *Thinking the unthinkable: the immigration myth exposed*. London: I.B. Tauris.

Hayek, F.A.v., 1991. *Economic freedom*. Oxford: Basil Blackwell.

Hayter, T., 2001. *Open borders*. London: Pluto Press.

Marx, K., 1976. *Capital I*. Harmondsworth: Penguin.

Milanovic, B., 2007. Globalization and inequality. *In*: D. Held and A. Kaya, eds. *Global inequality: patterns and explanations*. Cambridge and Malden, MA: Polity, 26–49.

Munck, R. ed., 2009. *Globalisation and migration: new issues, new politics*. London and New York: Routledge.

Münz, R., Straubhaar, T., Vadean, F. and Vadean, N., 2007. *What are the migrants' contributions to employment and growth? A European approach.* HWWI Policy Papers 3–3. Hamburg: Hamburg Institute of International Economics.

Nayar, D., 1994. International labour movements, trade flows and migration transitions: a theoretical perspective. *Asian and pacific migration journal,* 3 (1), 31–47.

Organisation for Economic Cooperation and Development [OECD], 2007. *International migration outlook: annual report 2007.* Paris: Organisation for Economic Cooperation and Development.

Oxfam, 2002. *Rigged rules and double standards: trade, globalisation, and the fight against poverty.* Oxford: Oxfam.

Passel, J.S. and Cohn, D.V., 2009. *A Portrait of unauthorized immigrants in the United States.* Washington, DC: Pew Hispanic Center.

Passel, J.S. and Cohn, D.V., 2011. *Unauthorized immigrant population: National and State trends 2010.* Washington, DC: Pew Hispanic Center. Available from: http://pewhispanic.org/reports/report.php?ReportID=133 [Accessed 15 July 2011].

Pécoud, A. and de Guchteneire, P., eds., 2007. *Migration without borders: essays on the free movement of people.* Paris: UNESCO.

Phillips, N., 2011a. Migration and the global economic crisis. *In*: N. Phillips, ed. *Migration in the global political economy.* Boulder, Co: Lynne Rienner.

Phillips, N., ed., 2011b. *Migration in the global political economy.* Boulder, Co: Lynne Rienner.

Pieke, F.N., 2011. Immigrant China. *Modern China,* 38 (1), 40–77.

Piguet, É., Pécoud, A. and de Guchteneire, P. eds., 2011. *Migration and climate change.* Cambridge: Cambridge University Press for UNESCO.

Polanyi, K., 2001. *The great transformation.* Boston, MA: Beacon Press.

Portes, A., Guarnizo, L.E., and Landolt, P., 1999. The study of transnationalism: pitfalls and promise of an emergent research field. *Ethnic and racial studies,* 22 (2), 217–237.

Reyneri, E., 2001. *Migrants' involvement in irregular employment in the mediterranean countries of the European Union.* Geneva: International Labour Organization.

Salt, J. and Clarke, J., 2000. International migration in the UNECE region: patterns, trends, policies. *International social science journal,* 52 (165), 313–328.

Saunders, D., 2011. *Arrival city: how the largest migration in history is reshaping our world.* London: Windmill Books.

Sen, A., 2001. *Development as freedom.* Oxford: Oxford University Press.

Skeldon, R., 2006. Interlinkages between internal and international migration and development in the Asian region. *Population, space and place,* 12, 15–30.

Stiglitz, J.E., 2002. *Globalization and its discontents.* London: Penguin.

Straubhaar, T., 2002. Towards a general agreement on movements of people (GAMP). *Journal of international peace and organization,* 77 (1–2), 71–96.

Straubhaar, T. and Zimmermann, K., 1992. *Towards a European migration policy.* London: Centre for Economic Policy Research.

Swan, W.T. 2010. Australia to 2050: future challenges. Intergenerational report. Barton: Productivity Commission.

United Nations Department of Economic and Social Affairs [UNDESA], 2009. *Trends in international migrant stock: the 2008 revision.* New York: United Nations Department of Economic and Social Affairs, Population Division.

United Nations Development Programme [UNDP], 2009. *Human development report 2009: overcoming barriers: human mobility and development.* New York: United Nations Development Programme. Available from: http://hdr.undp.org/en/reports/global/hdr2009/ [Accessed 5 December 2009].

Vasta, E. and Castles, S. eds., 1996. *The teeth are smiling: the persistence of racism in multicultural Australia.* Sydney: Allen and Unwin.

Appendix

Table 1 UN figures on population, international migrants and refugees.

	Year	World Billions	World Per cent	MDCs Billions	MDCs Per cent	LDCs Billions	LDCs Per cent
Population	1990	5.3	100	1.1	22	4.1	78
Population	1995	5.7	100	1.2	21	4.5	79
Population	2000	6.1	100	1.2	18	4.9	80
Population	2005	6.5	100	1.2	19	5.3	81
Population	2010	6.9	100	1.2	18	5.7	82
		Millions	Per cent	Millions	Per cent	Millions	Per cent
Int. migrants	1990	156	100	82	53	73	47
Int. migrants	1995	166	100	94	57	72	43
Int. migrants	2000	178	100	104	59	74	41
Int. migrants	2005	195	100	117	60	78	40
Int. migrants	2010	214	100	128	60	86	40
		Millions	Per cent	Millions	Per cent	Millions	Per cent
Refugees	1990	18.4	100	2.0	11	16.5	89
Refugees	1995	18.5	100	3.9	21	14.6	79
Refugees	2000	15.6	100	3.1	20	12.5	80
Refugees	2005	13.9	100	2.5	18	11.3	82
Refugees	2010	16.3	100	2.4	14	14.0	85

Notes: Data are at mid-year for each year.
Int. migrants, international migrants, defined as persons who have lived outside their country of origin for at least a year; MDCs, more developed countries; LDCs, less developed countries.
Source: Own calculations from UN Population Division (UNDESA 2009).

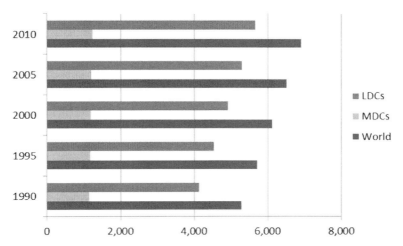

Figure 1 World population at mid-year (estimated: millions).
Source: UN Population Division (UNDESA 2009).

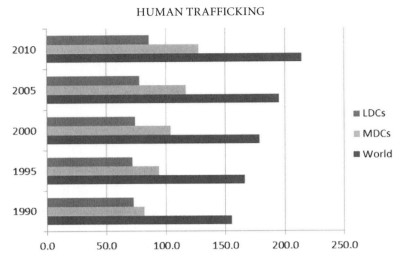

Figure 2 World migrant stock (estimated: millions).
Source: UN Population Division (UNDESA 2009).

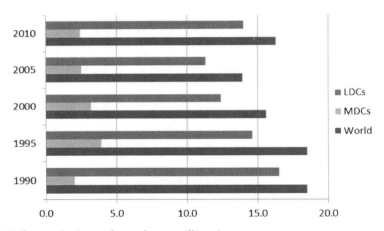

Figure 3 Refugees (estimated numbers: millions).
Source: UN Population Division (UNDESA 2009).

The Political and Economic Transition from Communism and the Global Sex Trafficking Crisis: A Case Study of Moldova

Jenny Bryson Clark & Denese McArthur

This paper will investigate the effects of political and economic transition from communism to a greater market system and its impact upon the increase of sex trafficking in Moldova. Moldova is considered to be one of the most affected 'source countries' for trafficked women and children because of differential degrees of economic and political liberalization in different regions of the country. Observations of both the incidence of trafficking and government responsiveness to the issue from Moldova yield useful insights into the question of whether structural changes within the political and economic system decrease social stability and create an environment in which trafficking will flourish.

The issue of human trafficking has drawn the attention of the world's public at levels not seen since the abolitionist era of the early nineteenth century. Politicians, policy-makers, the media, and international agencies have weighed in on the causes and implications of the most recent wave of global slavery, which is largely considered to have become truly prolific following the end of the cold war. With the breakup of the Soviet Union in 1991 and subsequent transitions of its member states and associated republics toward more open political and economic structures, the movement of people across borders and cultures evolved from relatively isolated occurrences to a massive mobilization of unprecedented scale. Borders that had once been both secure and strictly enforced became porous, and smuggling was rampant. What was once exotic became commonplace. Within this context, criminal networks evolved to exploit the weaknesses within both state and society. By the end of the decade, the term 'white slavery' had been resurrected and was being used to describe the proliferation of trafficking of (mostly) women and girls out of the east and into the more 'developed' world for the purpose of sexual exploitation and domestic servitude. The commodification of people, though not new, became a global issue of massive proportions.

As national and international actors and agencies scrambled to design and then coordinate policies to combat the problem of human trafficking (a broad term encompassing labor and sex trafficking as well as less-common practices), scholars and humanitarian workers joined them in analysing the likely causes (see Hughes 2000; Aronowitz 2001; Paci 2002; Malarek 2004; Corrin 2005; Tavcer 2006; Kara 2009; Mahmoud and Trebisch 2010; Shelley 2010; Chakarova 2011). It soon became apparent that a significant percentage of the victims of the global sex trade were from Moldova. Why the disproportionate number of Moldovan victims? In this paper, we present the first tests of a model of human trafficking that focuses on the intersection between gendered effects of economic liberalization and sociopolitical transformation to explain the cross-national variation in patterns of victimization. The analyses will demonstrate that the economic forces which make people vulnerable to exploitation, combined with weak or absent institutional safeguards for their protection, have turned Moldova into one of the biggest source countries for traffickers and their victims in the region. The paper proceeds in four parts. In the following section, we discuss the effects of the post-cold war transition on the economic and social systems of the former Soviet states and identify several factors that may explain why Moldova has suffered comparatively more than every other Eastern European country. Next, we provide evidence of the scope of the trafficking problem and address the systemic conditions that perpetuate the practice, paying particular attention to the gendered effects of poverty and inequality. Then, we discuss the linkages between poverty, migration, and trafficking and explain the short- and long-term impacts that globalization has had on these issues. Finally, we examine the current structural and legal mechanisms for eliminating human trafficking in Moldova and identify the social, economic, and political forces that impede or facilitate progress toward this goal.

Economic Shockwaves of the Soviet Collapse

To some, the rapid growth of human trafficking in Eastern Europe is emblematic of the worst aspects of capitalism. Economic globalization has transformed the international division of labor in a way that has led to a deepening of poverty across the former Soviet empire. As shown in Table 1, standard indicators of economic strength and stability (including gross domestic product [GDP], consumer price inflation, and unemployment levels) all reflect the intensity of the crisis in the early years of the transition period.

Moldova suffered the steepest decline of any of the satellite states. In the initial phase (1991—1996), economic output contracted by 64 per cent from its 1989 level, ultimately hitting its lowest point in 1999 (the year the Russian economy collapsed) at 33 per cent (see Figure 1).

As the Moldovan economy depended predominantly on agricultural exports to Russia, falling food prices pushed the already frail economy into devastation (Scanlan 2002; Cornia 2006). The secession of Transdniestria in 1992 compounded Moldova's economic woes further as most of the country's industrial complex was situated in this region. It is worth noting that the two most precipitous drops in productivity occurred in 1992 and 1994, when severe flooding struck Moldova's agricultural heartland, which is the source of almost half of the country's GDP (Cornia 2006). Production has been steadily increasing since 1999, though it has yet to reach 60 per cent of its pretransition figure. Inflation was extremely high in the period immediately after the breakup of the Soviet Union, averaging 639 per cent over the 1991—1994 period. It has been estimated that the interaction between falling economic output and hyperinflation, combined with a sharp rise in income inequality (see Figure 2), caused poverty rates in Moldova to reach 65—70 per cent by the year 1995 (Cornia 2006).

Driven in part by the subsequent Russian economic crisis, the number of people living below the poverty line reached 80 per cent of the population in 2001 (UNDP 2003). In order to assist former Soviet republics with their transition to western-style market economies, the International Monetary Fund (IMF, 2012) pushed measures calling for opening of markets to foreign investments (Klein 2007; Kara 2009). The move from a centralized economy also prompted drastic reductions in government support for education, health, and social programs (Hughes 2000, United Nations 2000; Milanovic 2002; Scanlan 2002; Corrin 2005; Klein 2007; Kara 2009; Clark 2012). The loss of social safety nets was felt particularly strongly by women, young people, and the rural poor (Blum 2008: 87).

Table 2 presents a comparison of economic inequality across the former Soviet republics and affiliated states, incorporating data from 1986 to 2009. Prior to the political upheavals of the period, Moldova (like its formerly socialist neighbors) had comparatively little inequality of income (Atkinson and Micklewright 1992). As with most other countries in the region, Moldova enjoyed a relatively high level of human development and social welfare, although evidence of cultural capital redistribution was apparent (Konrad and Szelenyi 1979). The centralized social, economic, and

Table 1 Select economic indicators.

	1990	1991	1992	1993	1994	1995	1996	1997	1998	1999	2000	2001	2002	2003	2004	2005	2006	2007	2008	2009	2010	2011
GDP index	98	80	57	56	39	38	36	37	34	33	34	36	38	41	44	48	50	51	55	51	56	59
GDP growth	-2.8	-16.2	-29.2	-1.1	-30.7	-0.9	-5.0	1.8	-6.3	-3.2	2.3	6.3	8.1	6.9	7.7	7.8	5.1	3.3	8	-5.8	7.2	6.5
Inflation	5.6	162.0	1276.1	788.5	329.6	30.2	23.5	11.8	7.7	39.3	31.3	9.8	5.3	11.7	12.5	12.0	12.8	12.4	12.8	0.01	7.4	7.6
Unemployed	*	*	15	14.1	20.6	24.5	23.4	28	32	34.9	28.9	27.6	24	19.7	21	21.7	20.4	18.9	17.8	*	*	*
-Female	*	*	9.1	8.9	12.9	16.1	15.9	17.7	19	21.6	17	14	12.3	9.4	9.3	10.4	10.8	10.6	10.5	*	*	*
-Male	*	*	5.9	5.2	7.7	8.4	7.5	10.3	13	13.3	11.9	13.6	11.7	10.3	11.7	11.3	9.6	8.3	7.3	*	*	*
Remittances	*	*	*	*	*	1.0	3.1	1.3	1.2	0.6	52.6	80.2	101.6	152	221.4	395.1	602.8	842.3	1046	635.2	608.5	701.4
-% GDP	*	*	*	*	*	0.07	0.22	0.09	0.09	0.05	4.08	5.87	6.89	9.68	13.12	21.78	31.72	42.99	49.55	32.01	28.63	31.01

*Data unavailable.

GDP index (1989 = 100) – European Bank for Reconstruction and Development, various years.

GDP per capita growth (annual %) – World Bank.

Inflation, consumer prices (year-to-year %) – World Bank.

Unemployment, total (% of total labor force) – ILO.

Unemployment, female (% of female labor force) – ILO.

Unemployment, male (% of male labor force) – ILO.

Workers' remittances, receipts (current US$) – World Bank.

Workers' remittances expressed as a percent of GDP – World Bank.

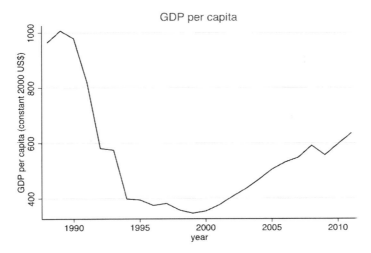

Figure 1 Moldovan economic output, 1988 – 2011.

political controls imposed by the Soviet Union guaranteed stable employment for all its citizens. Social security, health care, and many other social programs were provided for all citizens along with housing and day care. With extensive social investment during the communist administration, literacy rates were almost universal and above other countries with comparable levels of per capita (Economic Survey of Europe 2004). High levels of social expenditure and low wage differentials meant that the distribution of income within the Central and Eastern Europe (CEE) countries was significantly more egalitarian than most market economies.

The end of the cold war also paved the way for an opening of new markets in the former Soviet Union and satellite states and provided new sources of cheap labor.

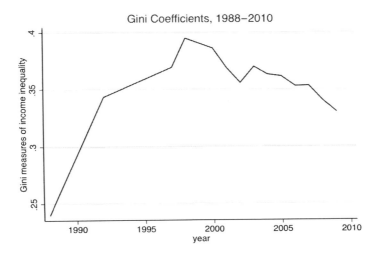

Figure 2 Gini coefficients (based on equality of income).

Table 2 Gini coefficients for select Eastern European nations.

	1986[a]	1992/1993	1998/1999	2002/2003	2008/2009
Armenia	.251		.360	.338	.309
Azerbaijan	.280			.365	.337
Georgia	.273		.373	.403	.413
Kyrgyz Republic	.254	.537	.360	.317	.373
Moldova	.240	.343	.395	.369	.353
Romania		.255	.294	.315	.312
Russia	.221	.484	.375	.357	.423
Tajikistan	.256		.290	.326	.308
Ukraine	.233	.257		.283	.275
Uzbekistan	.256		.453	.346	

Gini measure of economic inequality, with higher values representing greater inequality.
[a]Data are from Alexeev and Gaddy, 1991. Remaining data are from the World Bank.

This coincided with the existing trend toward decentralized production that had resulted from increased trade liberalization, and which was fuelling international market competition and an intensified drive to reduce labor costs (Beneria 2001). The result was that many businesses sought to transfer their more labor-intensive processes to countries where wages were low (Wood 1994; Beneria 2001). An examination of shifts in Moldova's economic system after 1990 (in Figure 3) reveals an immediate drop in industrial production coinciding with an increase in the agricultural sector. Both trends are likely the result of deregulation of the labor

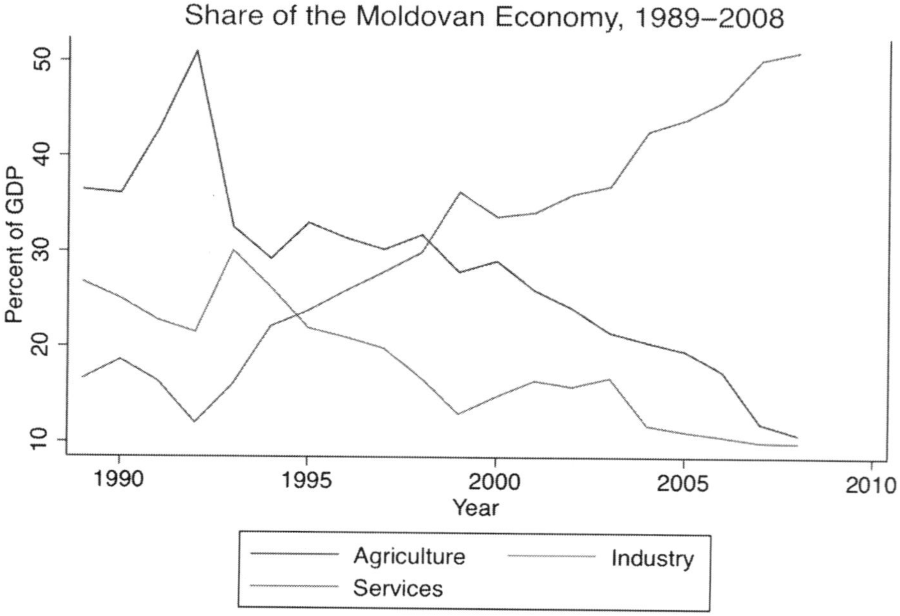

Figure 3 Moldovan economic market (by sector).

market and more options for workers to move about the region. By 1995, however, changes in the relative strengths of the three major economic sectors had begun to irrevocably alter the dynamics of the labor market. Industry's share of the economy declined rapidly, as did that of the agricultural sector. The role of the service industry took on new importance. These patterns would prevail (with only brief interruptions in 1999) until today (Figure 4).

While Moldova is hardly unique among the postsocialist states in terms of the challenges faced as a result of the shift away from a managed economy, the country has experienced a confluence of circumstances that have drastically increased its citizens' vulnerability to human trafficking. To better understand the forces at work in suppressing significant industrial development, it is useful to consider the nature of Moldova's business market, particularly in the aftermath of the Soviet collapse. Economic reforms have been slow and the business environment is poor. Its foreign investment is lowest in South Eastern Europe (SSEI Guide 2006). Beginning in 1991, security within the newly independent states quickly crumbled, government corruption became ubiquitous, and organized criminal networks infiltrated many segments of the society.

The Republic of Moldova is recognized as a major source country for trafficking in persons (Organization for Security and Cooperation in Europe [OSCE] December 2003: 9; *Trafficking in Persons Report* 3 June 2005). Moldova is the poorest nation in the former Eastern bloc and one of the poorest nations globally. Moldova also ranks 115 of 177 in the UNDP Human Development Index in 2005 and 111 out of 187 in 2011 (UNDP 2011). Significantly, Moldova has one of the youngest populations in Europe, with almost 30 per cent of the population under the age of 18. Due to their increased mobility, and motivated by declining opportunities to pursue higher education (as a result of cuts to government funding for education subsidies), young people in general have been more willing to migrate, both internally and abroad.

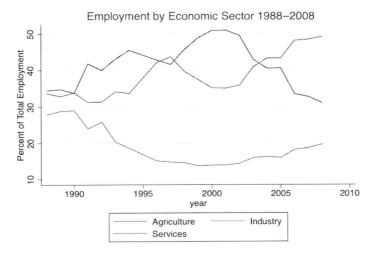

Figure 4 Employment rates by sector of the economy, 1988–2008.

(Not coincidentally, traffickers also tend to target young people.) The breakup of the collective farms of the Soviet era increased unemployment rates among the rural communities, and many small towns suffered when their sole industries failed (Orlova 2004). During the upheaval of the early 1990s, Moldova experienced the worst population decrease and migration flow of any former Soviet Republic, with between 600,000 and 1 million of its citizens migrating overseas in search of better employment opportunities, an estimated one quarter of the population, between 1991 and 2003 (International Organization of Migration [IOM] 2000; UNDP National Human Development Report 2000; Limanowska 2002; Jandi 2003; American Bar Association [ABA] and Central European and Eurasian Law Initiative [CEELI] 2006; Gorlich and Trebesch 2008). The economy of Moldova has grown dependent upon the income sent home from workers who have migrated abroad, with annual remittances equal to almost 50 per cent of GDP in 2008 (see Table 1, rows 7–8).

Corruption and organized crime are a systemic problem in Moldova. Corruption is deeply embedded in virtually every aspect of law enforcement. On Transparency International's corruption scale, Moldova scored a 2.6 (out of 10) in 2000, placing it among countries with the high levels of corruption. Moldova ranked last on the aggregated quality of governance index (Transparency International 2009). Moldova is also plagued with problems from its breakaway territory of Transdniester, which poses unique challenges to its security and that of the other countries in the region. Transdniester suffers from an almost complete absence of the rule of law (although the situation is improving) and is described as a 'major focal point of major smuggling rings' (Chubashenko 2005). Transdniester is also known to be a haven for Russian and Ukrainian organized crime syndicates, with the lack of border security being one of the more significant obstacles to political and economic stability.

The Scope of Human Trafficking in Moldova

In recent years, trafficking in persons has emerged as a salient social issue: its scale is significant and has commanded the attention of governments, nongovernmental organizations, academics, journalists, and civil society. The International Organization of Labor (ILO) estimates that there are 12.3 million people worldwide in forced, bonded, labor, and sexual servitude. An estimated 2.5 million are victims of human trafficking of which two-thirds are women and children trafficked into commercial sexual exploitation (ILO 2005). The IOM estimates that between 800,000 and two million women and children are trafficked across international borders annually (IOM 2006), and it is estimated that between 175,000 −and 200,000 are trafficked annually in Eastern Europe and Central Asia (ILO 2005, United Nations Population Fund 2006 in Mahmoud and Trebresch 2010). Human trafficking is arguably the world's fastest growing criminal enterprise. The ILO estimates that sexual and labor exploitation yields US$ 32 billion in annual profits, while the global sex trade rakes in US$ 12 billion a year (Malarek 2004; ILO 2005; Kara 2009).

As previously mentioned, Moldova has been the source country for a disproportionate number of trafficking victims. Although data are not available from the cold war and the earliest phase of the transition period, it is believed that the problem of sex trafficking likely accelerated in the absence of traditional security structures following the Soviet breakup (Blum 2008: 86). The dramatic surge in migration following the 1998–1999 economic crisis also contributed significantly. By the late 1990s, the extent of the trafficking problem had grown to the point where several nongovernmental organizations (NGOs) and victims' services providers had set-up operations in Moldova.

Investigating human trafficking is impeded by numerous well-known challenges that, while well documented, are still worth noting. Statistics on trafficking vary considerably due to inconsistencies on definitions of trafficking, methods of obtaining data, and the clandestine nature of organized crime. As sex trafficking is an illegal enterprise, statistics can be hard to obtain and it is likely that cases are often underreported. This limits our ability to conduct sound empirical research. States frequently deny the existence or extent of trafficking within their borders, and the reports of NGOs and human rights organizations are not always reliable. Many simply report what they are told by the victims of trafficking, and their primary focus is on countering government denials, especially when there is sufficient evidence of widespread trafficking (Bales 2004; Kara 2009). NGO statistics are usually a direct result of their efforts to protect and care for trafficked women survivors, which include those who independently seek help in addition to those brought to their attention by official sources. Incentives exist to inflate the numbers in order to draw the attention of political leaders.

The Feminization of Poverty and Migration

While the study of human trafficking has garnered much interest, less attention has been directed at some of the economic aspects of trafficking, including globalization and the spread of free market policies that have resulted in large migration flows. The limited options for legal migration across Moldova's borders have fostered a breeding ground for smuggling networks and other criminal entities. These groups have capitalized on and profited from vulnerability and individuals' need to migrate in order to work or even survive (Jordan 2004; Kara 2009; Shelley 2010). Women and children tend to be particularly vulnerable to the threats posed by the multibillion-dollar trafficking industry.

The effects of restructured labor markets and increases in economic inequality vary according to predictable factors such as gender, race, and class. Women, in particular, have been disproportionately affected by skyrocketing unemployment, high inflation, and decrease in government spending on social services (Erturk 2009).

Economic downturns and shifts in labor patterns tend to have a greater impact on women. The uneven impact of free-marketization has had a dramatic effect on Moldova reinforcing the cyclic nature of feminized poverty. Marcoux (1998) notes that of 1300 million persons worldwide living in poverty, 70 per cent is women. This percentage is especially high in transition countries, such as Moldova, and postconflict areas. The loss of jobs for women in Moldova has been three times that of men (UNICEF 2000). According to Kligman and Limoncelli (2005), male unemployment dropped from 37 per cent to 32 per cent, while unemployment for Moldovan women increased from 62 per cent to 67 per cent between 1994 and 1997 (Minnesota Advocates for Human Rights 2000 in Kligman and Limoncelli 2005).

The term 'feminization of poverty' refers to a change in poverty levels that is biased against female heads of household. The abandonment of Soviet-mandated equality caused traditional paternalistic values to return to Moldova, which combined with deteriorating economic conditions have led to a situation where women are more likely to fall into poverty than their male counterparts. Gender inequality exacerbates poverty and endangers the prospect of economic growth and human development. Cuts in welfare, education, and health services, combined with the male breadwinner ethos, have placed enormous burdens on women. Women are frequently the first to lose their jobs or have to compromise their jobs to look after children or elders. Despite the level of educational equality prior to the Soviet collapse, today's women are employed in jobs that are below their level of skill and which result in lower rates of pay (Kremen 1990).

Domestic violence has also increased in Moldova. Domestic violence is not a new phenomenon; however, reported incidents have increased within the last decade. The Ministry of Internal Affairs compiles annual reports on homicides and grave corporal injuries, but as La Strada (a Moldovan NGO) notes, these are just 'dry numbers' and based only on reported incidences. As such, the numbers are likely to be vastly understated. Based on reports from NGOs operating in Moldova, La Strada reports that 41 per cent of women were affected by family violence during their lifetime, and that 20 per cent of women cannot make any decisions without consent of their husband (La Strada Express 2008). Numerous Moldovan trafficking victims interviewed cite domestic violence, rape, beatings, and psychological abuse at the hands of their husbands, fathers, and uncles as the reason they seek alternative work in other countries (Kara 2009). Seven out of 10 sex trafficking victims that La Strada has assisted in Moldova since 2000 cite domestic violence as the primary factor in accepting proposals to travel abroad (La Strada Express 2008).

Poverty is one of the main driving forces of migration. The lack of economic opportunity and the desire for a better life abroad is one of the strongest push factors guiding immigration and puts millions of people at risk of exploitation (Kligman and Limoncelli 2005; World Bank 2005; Mahmoud and Trebesch 2010; Shelley 2010; Calvani and Jung 2012). The large potential gains from migration have generated an unprecedented demand for legal migration to richer countries. This is exceedingly evident in countries like Mexico, which has high seasonal and long-term out-migration and increased levels of trafficking (Boltvinich 2000; Acharya 2006; Clark 2012; Payan 2012; Tiano 2012).

Like Mexico, Moldova has both seasonal and permanent migrations. In recent years, the number of men migrating has increased from 21 per cent in 2010 to 29 per cent in 2012. According to studies by the IOM, there are generally four categories of migrants from Moldova. The two largest groups are male construction workers in the Commonwealth of Independent States (CIS) (primarily Russia), the majority of whom are from rural areas and have low levels of education, and migrants to Israel and the European Union, over half of whom are women from rural areas. The other two groups are comprised of nonconstruction workers to the CIS (largely rural women with higher education) and predominantly rural women from rural areas who migrate to Turkey or Romania (IOM 2006, 2008; Erturk 2009).

Poverty has certainly been a major contributing factor of migration from rural areas to urban areas. A recent study conducted by the IOM using figures from the National Referral System for Assistance and Protection of Victims and Potential Victims of Trafficking (NRS) showed that most victims were single parents, children from boarding schools, or persons with low education, and/or from rural areas (IOM 2008). As agriculture has been hard hit, rural poverty has grown dramatically and for many rural populations, migration may be perceived as the only means for survival (IMF 2012 in Gorlich and Trebisch 2008; World Bank 2012).

The Moldovan capital, Chisinau, is characterized by hundreds of money exchanges and western union offices in a country with essentially no tourist trade, a fact that suggests the importance of and dependence upon foreign remittances to the Moldovan economy. With most labor markets in the developed nations closed off, there is only a very limited supply of legal opportunities for migration. The clandestine nature and operation of illegal of migration networks and organizations that offer services such as passports, visas, border crossings, and employment opportunities are very similar to how human trafficking networks operate. Human smuggling is highly lucrative and numerous studies have exposed the issues surrounding human smuggling, undocumented migration, and criminal networks that facilitate the movement of people across borders (Laczko 2005; Farrell *et al.* 2007; Shelley 2010; Tiano 2012). Human smuggling can turn into human trafficking at any stage and the links between migration and trafficking are becoming more apparent (Friebel and Guriev 2006; Tavcer 2006; Mahmoud and Trebesch 2010). Many observers look to the example of other transition states that have integrated or are in the process of aligning with the European Union. Successful neighbors such as Bulgaria and Romania have seen immediate benefits from simplified border crossings and increased economic prospects.

An increase in immigration is one of the main indicators of human trafficking Women seeking employment overseas are tricked and sold into prostitution and trafficked. While exact figures remain unknown, the ILO estimates that more than 200,000 people from Eastern Europe and Central Asia have been trafficked (ILO 2005). Some insights into the scale of the problem can be gleaned from official programs that aim to assist returning victims of trafficking. Between January 2000 and May 2003, a total of 1056 victims of trafficking were repatriated to Moldova with the assistance of the International Organization for Migration, according to the IOM counter-trafficking office in Chisinau.

Gender and minority disenfranchisement that millions of women face across the globe meant women and children were the hardest hit during times of socioeconomic crisis and have been the most heavily trafficked. In 1997, an estimated 175,000 women and girls were trafficked from CEE and CIS into Western Europe, and furthermore 120,000 women and children are trafficked annually specifically into the European Union mostly through the Balkans (OSCE 2003). The trafficking of women for the purpose of sexual exploitation in Europe has undergone a boom in productivity and exploitation since the collapse of the communist system in the former Soviet Bloc and elsewhere in Eastern Europe. The flight of many of Moldova's adult population has left behind social orphans (children who have parents but are working overseas) (Erturk 2009). A recent UNICEF State of the Children's report estimates that 29 per cent of children (approximately 8800) are without parents in Moldova (UNICEF 2009). These children are often left in boarding schools, orphanages, or with a relative. The orphan population of Moldova is overwhelming. The biggest danger occurs when orphans turn 16 and are discharged with no family, no social network, and little experience in life. Traffickers prey on such orphanages as recruitment areas for trafficking overseas (Malarek 2004).

Trafficking organizations operate similar to legitimate legal enterprises. Those operating in Moldova find and attract people willing to work abroad via advertisements in newspapers, the Internet, employment agencies travel agents, and sometimes recruiters, who are often former trafficking victims themselves. Most victims of trafficking in Moldova depart on a voluntary basis, lured with the promise of lucrative employment opportunities or sometimes marriage promises (ILO 2005). Friends or distant relatives recruit many victims. Laczko and Gramegna (2003) reported that over 60% of victims in South Eastern Europe are recruited by acquaintances mostly with the promise of jobs abroad. Women are also recruited through 'tourist companies' or 'employment abroad agencies.' Travel agencies that seem legal, but are operating illegally often recruit victims. Travel agencies provide people with visas and passports to destination countries. Together with illegal networks in destination countries these fronts help recruit. Most travel agencies in Moldova are unlicensed and often provide false visas and other travel documents. Hundreds of marriage agencies also exist and operate in Eastern Europe including Moldova (United Nations 2000, Demir 2010).

Most of the women who have been lured abroad with false job promises end up having to work under life-threatening conditions in brothels. Women are recruited mainly in the countryside, where they are first paid some $100 to come to Chisinau. They are later sold abroad for $300. The price goes up along the way, and when they are sold from Bucharest, the price is about $1,000. Many of the women are trafficked to and through Albania, Macedonia, and Kosovo, with Timisoa in Romania being the main transit point. As detected cases show, women are 'ordered' (one recent case concerned an 'order' of 50 women for bars in Istanbul) and promptly delivered on demand (Jandi 2003).

Globalization, Organized Crime, and Corruption

Lack of evidence makes it hard to determine whether true organized crime[1] is involved in the trafficking of people from Moldova, and to what extent. A study conducted by Finckenauer (2001) suggests that traffickers, in general, are young criminals, attracted by the prospect of earning easy money. Human trafficking carries relatively low risks and therefore might easily attract the attention of local criminal enterprises. It seems that traffickers can range from enterprisers with no previous criminal background, to mixed groups of families, local criminal groups, to sophisticated organized groups that operate both nationally and internationally. Evidence does seem to suggest that true organized crime might play a secondary role in trafficking of persons as debt collectors, charging a fee to permit trafficking in their territory (Finckenauer 2001).

While globalization has led to unprecedented increases in migration and trafficking, it has also enabled and facilitated the traffickers, allowing them to operate more easily. Economic liberalization of the former Soviet Republic has led to a weakening the rule of law, which has allowed the black market economy and corruption to flourish. Corruption results in distorted economic policies that benefit elites and limit economic development thus hindering further marginalized, vulnerable persons (Malarek 2004, 2009; Tavcer 2006). Corruption in Moldova is systemic, pervasive, and is well documented (Transparency International 2002; ABA and CEELI 2006; TRaCCC 2006). The worst sectors affected by corruption are the judiciary, police, and customs services (Transparency International 2002). Moldova Civil servants such as border patrol agents, police, and customs officials facilitate traffickers by taking bribes to increase their low salaries, which are often not enough to live on. Bribery and money laundering is widespread, almost 60 per cent of the general public in Moldova report paying 'extra fees' to government officials (Mann and Dolea 2006). Increased speed and ease of money movement also makes it easier for traffickers to launder their profits and operate with impunity. Globalization has also facilitated low cost, speedy communications that help traffickers operate. Websites advertise sex tourism overseas and child pornography, and mail-order brides provide a discreet cover for trafficking.

The absence of an impartial and independent judiciary compounds the situation. Compromised judicial systems have allowed the black market to flourish and the government remains reluctant to acknowledge its role in prevention and prosecution of trafficking in women (Mann and Dolea 2006). Despite the fact that Moldova has made considerable efforts in its passage of anti-trafficking legislation in 2003 followed by the Law on Preventing and Combating Trafficking in Human Beings 2005, and the National Plan for Prevention and Combating of Trafficking in Human Beings (most recent 2010 – 2011 not legally binding), corruption remains one of the biggest barriers in the fight against sex trafficking in Moldova. According to the US State Department in Chisinau, in 2004 there were only 16 convictions for trafficking in persons, 75 for pimping, and 7 for trafficking of children. Of those cases, only 16 involved prison time (mostly less than two years) (Kara 2009). Due to its lack of enforcement of anti-trafficking laws, Moldova fell to a Tier 2 watch list in 2007 and fell to Tier 3 in 2008 (US State Department TIP Report 2007, 2008). In 2008, the US sent a team of federal law enforcement trainers and Federal Bureau of Investigation agents to provide anti-trafficking related training. After the training, an agent noted that new cars were often given to Moldovan officials out of TIP funds. In 2009, several high-ranking members of the Interior Ministry were removed from their positions because of their personal involvement in human trafficking organizations. None have been prosecuted.

Summary and Conclusions

The transition from a planned economy to economic liberalization has had tremendous implications on the economy and social structure of Moldova. The consequences of shifting economic priorities have limited the ability of many women to improve their situation. Poverty and lack of opportunity continue to be driving forces for many women to embark on risky migration options for more lucrative employment opportunities abroad. The feminization of poverty, declining public health care, and diminishing or absent social safety nets combined with new forms of criminal enterprises have increased the number of women and girls becoming victims of trafficking. While the economic climate has improved somewhat in recent years, inequality is actually increasing. Efforts to address trafficking remain piecemeal and are often ineffective because they do not address the deeper factors that promote trafficking. Attention to these factors must be a priority. Within the current political climate, this is unlikely to occur. While politicians are divided among two camps – those interested in pursuing eventual membership with the EU, and those who prefer aligning the country with Russian interests – consistent focus on resolving issues of poverty and inequality will be difficult to achieve. Unfortunately, as these conditions persist, the supply of trafficking victims will remain intolerably high.

Note

[1]   Crime may be organized, but not necessarily fit the criteria of 'organized crime.' While much criminal activity in the trafficking of persons may be organized that does not infer that organized crime such as the Russian Mafia are necessarily involved.

Works Cited

Acharya, A., 2006. International migration and trafficking of Mexican women to the United States. *In*: K. Beeks and D. Emir, eds. *Trafficking and the global sex industry*. Lanham, MD: Lexington Books, 21–32.

American Bar Association – Central European and Eurasian Law Institute, 2006. *CEDAW assessment tool report for Moldova.*

Aronowitz, A., 2001. *Human trafficking, human misery: the global trade in human beings.* Westport, CT: Praeger.

Atkinson, A. and Micklewright, J., 1992. *Economic transformations in Eastern Europe and the distribution of income.* Cambridge: Cambridge University Press.

Bales, K., 2004. *Disposable people: new slavery in the global economy.* Berkeley, CA: University of California Press.

Beneria, L., 2001. *Changing employment patterns and the informalization of jobs: general trends and gender dimensions.* Geneva: International Labour Office.

Blum, L., 2008. *Sex trafficking and political discourse: a case study of the perceptions and definition of the problem and its victims in Moldova.* Doctoral Dissertation. University of Arkansas.

Boltvinik, J. 2000. *Debate, desigualida y pobreza.* La Journada. April 28. Mexico City.

Calvani, S. and Jung, O. (in collaboration with Vittoria Luda di Cortemiglia), 2012. Migration; the forgotten link in the nexus between freedom from want and freedom from fear. *In*: Tiano and Murphy-Aguilar, eds. *Borderline slavery: Mexico, the United States and the human trade.* Surrey: Ashgate Press.

Chakarova, M., 2011. The price of sex. A documentary distributed by WMM.

Chubashenko, D., 2005. EU opens border mission to halt Moldova smuggling, *Reuters*, 30 November.

Clark, J., 2012. Sex trafficking in Mexico: the Nexus between poverty, violence against women, and gender inequalities. *In*: S.B. Tiano and M. Murphy-Aguilar eds. *Borderline slavery: Mexico, United States and the human trade.* Surrey: Ashgate.

Cornia, G.A., 2006. *Poverty, inequality and policy affecting vulnerable groups in Moldova.* Innocenti Working Paper No. 2006–2005. Florence: UNICEF Innocenti Research Centre.

Corrin, C., 2005. Transitional road for traffic: analysing trafficking in women from and through Central and Eastern Europe. *Europe-Asia studies*, 57 (4), 543–560.

Demir, O., 2010. Methods of Sex Trafficking: Findings of a Case Study in Turkey. *Global crime*, 11 (3), 314–335.

Economic Survey of Europe, 2004. *United nations economic commission for Europe, No. 1.*

Erturk, Y., 2009. Promotion and protection of all human rights, civil, political, economic, social and cultural rights, including the right to development. *Report of the special rapporteur on violence against women, its causes and consequences.* New York: United Nations.

Farrell, A., McDevitt, J. and Fahy, S., 2007. *Understanding and improving law enforcement responses to human trafficking.* Washington, DC: National Institute of Justice.

Finckenauer, J., 2001. Russian transnational organized crime and trafficking. *In*: D. Kyle and R. Koslowski eds. *Global human smuggling: comparative perspectives.* Baltimore: John Hopkins University Press.

Friebel, G. and Guriev, S., 2006. Smuggling humans: a theory of debt-financed migration. *Journal of the European economic association*, 4, 1085–1111.

Gorlich, D. and Trebisch, C., 2008. Seasonal migration and networks – evidence on Moldova's labour exodus. *Review of world economics*, 144 (1), 107–133.

Hughes, D., 2000. The Natasha Trade; the transitional shadow market of trafficking in women. *Journal of international affairs*, 53 (2), p. 625.

International Labor Organization (ILO), 2005. *Employment in the informal economy in the Republic of Moldova.* Working Paper No. 41. ILO: Bureau of Statistics in collaboration with the Department for Statistics and Sociology of the Republic of Moldova.

International Monetary Fund (IMF), 2012. *Country report.* Moldova: IMF. Available from: http://www.imf.org/external/country/MDA/index.htm [Accessed 6 November 2012].

International Organization for Migration (IOM), 2000. Trafficking in women. Carmen Galiana, Civil Liberties Series LIBE 109 EN. March.

International Organization of Migration (IOM), 2006. *Human trafficking survey: Belarus, Bulgaria, Moldova, Romania and Ukraine.* Kyiv: Tetiana Sytnyk.

International Organization of Migration (IOM), 2008. *Migration in Moldova: a country profile.* Geneva: International Organization of Migration.

Jandi, M., 2003. *Moldova seeks stability amid mass emigration.* Vienna: Migration Policy Institute.

Jordan, A., 2004. *Human trafficking and globalization terror in the shadows: trafficking in money, weapons and people.* Washington, DC: Center for American Progress.

Kara, S., 2009. *Sex trafficking: inside the business of modern day slavery.* New York: Columbia University Press.

Kligman, G. and Limoncelli, S., 2005. Trafficking women after socialism: to, through, and from Eastern Europe. *Social politics: international studies in gender, state & society,* 12 (1), 118–140.

Klein, N., 2007. *The shock doctrine: the rise of disaster capitalism.* New York: Picador.

Konrad, G. and Szelenyi, I., 1979. *The Intellectuals on the road to class power.* Brighton: Harvester Press.

Kremen, E., 1990. Socialism: an escape from poverty? Women in European Russia. *In:* G. S. Goldberg and E. Kremen, eds. *The feminization of poverty: only in America?* New York: Praeger, 157–181.

Laczko, F., 2005. Data and research on human trafficking. *International migration,* 43 (1/2), 5–16.

Laczko, F. and Gramegna, M.A., 2003. Developing better indicators of human trafficking. *Brown journal of world affairs,* X (1), 179–194.

La Strada Express, 2008. *The problem of domestic violence in the Republic of Moldova – Reality and Perspectives.* La Strada: International Women's Human Rights Center. Available from: http://arhiva.lastrada.md/publicatii/ebook/La_Strada_express4_en_.pdf [Accessed 18 March 2014].

Limanowska, B., 2002. *Trafficking in human beings in Southeastern Europe.* Geneva: UNICEF/UNOHCHR/OSCE-ODIHR. June.

Mahmoud, T.O. and Trebesch, C., 2010. The economics of human trafficking and labor migration: micro-evidence from Eastern Europe. *Journal of comparative economics,* 38 (2), 173–188.

Malarek, V., 2004. *The Natashas.* New York: Arcade Publishing Press.

Malarek, V., 2009. Personal interview with Jenny Bryson Clark on 9 April 2009.

Mann, L.J. and Dolea, I., 2006. *OSCE Trial observation manual for the Republic of Moldova.* Chisinau: Organization for Security and Cooperation in Europe (OSCE)/ODIHR. 79; 182.

Marcoux, A., 1998. The feminization of poverty: claims, facts, and data needs. *Population and development review,* 24 (1), 131–139.

Milanovic, B., 2002. True world income distribution, 1988 and 1993: first calculations based on household surveys alone. *Economic journal,* 112 (476), 51–92.

Organization for Security and Cooperation in Europe (OSCE), 2003. *Report on trafficking in human beings in South Eastern Europe.* Warsaw: OSCE. Available from: http://polis.osce.org/library/f/3274/2220/OSCE-SRB-RPT-3274-EN-2220 [Accessed on 9 November 2012].

Orlova, A., 2004. From social dislocation to human trafficking. *Problems of post-communism,* 51 (6), 14–22.

Paci, P., 2002. *Gender in transition (Human development unit, Eastern Europe and Central Asia Region).* Washington, DC: World Bank.

Payan, T., 2012. Human trafficking and the US-Mexico border: reflections on a complex issue in a binational context. *In:* Tiano and Murphy-Aguilar, eds. *Borderline slavery: Mexico, the United States and the human trade.* Surrey: Ashgate.

Scanlan, S., 2002. *Report on trafficking from Moldova: irregular labor markets and restrictive migration policies in Western Europe.* IOM Report. Geneva: International Labor Organization.

SEEI Guide, 2006. *South Eastern Europe investment guide.* Available from: http://www.seeurope.net/files2/pdf/ig2006/At_Glance.pdf [Accessed 8 October 2010].

Shelley, L., 2010. *Human trafficking: a global perspective*. New York, NY: Cambridge University Press.

Tavcer, S., 2006. The trafficking of women for sexual exploitation: the situation from the Republic of Moldova to Western Europe. *Police practice and research*, 7 (2), 135–147.

Terrorism, Transnational Crime and Corruption Center (TraCCC), 2006. *The role of Russian business in foreign and security relations*. Fairfax, VA: Terrorism, Transnational Crime and Corruption Center.

Tiano, S., 2012. Human trafficking: a perfect storm of contributing factors. *In*: M. Murphy-Aguilar and S. Tiano, eds. *Borderline slavery: Mexico, United States, and the human trade*. Burlington, VT: Ashgate Press.

Transparency International, 2002. *Corruption perceptions index*. Available from: http://www.transparency.org/policy_surveys_indicies/cpi [Accessed 8 October 2010].

Transparency International, 2009. *Corruption perceptions index*. Available from: http://www.transparency.org/policy_surveys_indicies/cpi [Accessed 8 October 2010].

United Nations Development Programme (UNDP), 2000. *Moldova national human development report*. Chisinau, Moldova. Available from: http://www.undp.md/publications/NHDRs.shtml [Accessed December 2012].

United Nations Development Programme (UNDP), 2003. *Moldova national human development report*. Chisinau, Moldova. Available from: http://www.undp.md/publications/NHDRs.shtml [Accessed December 2012].

United Nations Development Programme (UNDP), 2011. *Moldova national human development report*. Chisinau, Moldova. Available from: http://www.undp.md/publications/NHDRs.shtml [Accessed December 2012].

UNICEF, 2000. *The situation of the world's children in the Republic of Moldova 2000–2001: assessment and analysis*. New York: UNICEF.

UNICEF, 2009. *The state of the world's children*. New York: UNICEF.

United Nations, 2000. *Common country assessment*. Moldova: United Nations.

United Nations, 2006. *Committee on the elimination of discrimination against women, thirty-sixth session*. Available from: http://www.un.org/womenwatch/daw/cedaw/cedaw25years/content/english/CONCLUDING_COMMENTS/Republic_of_Moldova/Moldova_CO-2-3.pdf [Accessed 8 October 2010].

United States Department of State, 2008. *Trafficking in persons report*. Washington, DC: United States Department of State. Available from: http://www.state.gov/g/tip/rls/tiprpt/2008/ [Accessed on 19 September 2010].

Wood, A., 1994. *North-South trade, employment and inequality: changing fortunes in a skill-driven world*. Oxford: Clarendon Press.

World Bank, 2005. *Growth, poverty and inequality: Eastern Europe and the former Soviet Union*. Available from: http://web.worldbank.org/WBSITE/EXTERNAL/COUNTRIES/ECAEXT/0,,contentMDK:20627214~pagePK:146736~piPK:146830~theSitePK:258599,00.html [Accessed 22 October 2010].

World Bank, 2012. *Moldova: poverty assessment*, Available from: http://data.worldbank.org/country/moldova [Accessed 2 November 2012].

Vulnerability to Human Trafficking among the Roma Population in Serbia: The Role of Social Exclusion and Marginalization

Sasha Poucki & Nicole Bryan

This paper examines vulnerability to human trafficking among the Roma population in Serbia. The inquiry is situated within the larger framework of discourse on human trafficking and seeks to analyse vulnerability and risk of victimization among members of a socially excluded, marginalized group. The inquiry also explores the potential for victimization to go unnoticed/unaddressed as a result of a number of factors, including structural/formal and informal mechanisms that reinforce cultural expectations and normalizations. The discussion is informed by the dynamics and complexities of victimization, including shifting patterns of victimization, the potential for participation in victimization and the role of resilience. The paper is sensitive to contested meanings of 'victimhood' and the role of agency, yet seeks to focus on vulnerability and risk of victimization among members of the Roma population in Serbia. The use of 'victim' in this paper is meant to be consistent with contextual power and agency.

The study of human trafficking and implementationc of anti-trafficking efforts have evolved considerably over the last 14 years. Since the United Nations' adoption of the Palermo Protocol in 2000,[1] attention to human trafficking among governmental and nongovernmental actors, including service providers, media and members of the business community, has grown steadily. A focus on victims and the importance of understanding factors that contribute to vulnerability and risk of victimization is part of this growth. While the late 1990s and early 2000s mark a period when governmental and non-governmental actors focused on the definition of human trafficking and codification of law for the purpose of prosecution, in more recent years the theme of *not criminalizing victims* has taken hold in anti-trafficking discourse. Understanding complex aspects of vulnerability and victimization, including shifting patterns and potential participation in victimization, is part of an effort to develop a more victim-centred approach. Special training on how to interact with victims to avoid re-traumatization is part of this effort. Victim-centred and rights-based approaches offer specific lenses through which to analyse vulnerability to human trafficking and risk of exploitation.

The US Department of State's Trafficking in Persons (TIP) Report reveals significant variation in the identification of victims and their treatment globally, including instances in which victims continue to be criminalized (2012). Despite considerable gaps in the evolution of anti-trafficking efforts globally, improvements can be observed in legislation and special training designed to help law enforcement better distinguish human trafficking, rather than conflate it with illegal prostitution, migration or other phenomena (US Department of State TIP Report 2012). Prevention and protection, nonetheless, remain a significant challenge. The dynamic nature of human trafficking and different ways it presents itself in contexts throughout the world adds to this challenge. The complexity of addressing underlying conditions and uprooting embedded, systemic inequities that sustain social injustice, exclusion and marginalization also play a role. Considerable disparity in the experience of victimization and development of effective methods of prevention and protection in different contexts for different risks – e.g. sex trafficking, organ trafficking, forced labour and others – contributes to the persistence of this challenge. Rescue and recovery raids, for example, at times fuelled by political pressure from foreign governments or other stakeholders to increase arrests and prosecution, receive criticism for sometimes causing more harm than good to victims or creating new victims by stripping independent sex workers of their rights (Kamler 2010). Awareness campaigns designed to contribute to prevention may fall short of achieving their goals, particularly in contexts where viable alternatives are scarce (UNODC 2008). Protection measures, including placing victims in custody, receive criticism for facilitating mistrust of law enforcement (Limanowska and Rosga 2004). These challenges notwithstanding, increasingly importance is placed on understanding the needs of victims and making sure proposed interventions, are designed with victims in mind and function to benefit and not harm victims (Latonero *et al.* 2011).[2] Within this context, the need for a more nuanced approach to understanding vulnerability, mitigating risk and improving prevention and protection is critical (UNODC 2008).

Analysis of root causes or underlying conditions contributing to vulnerability and risk of victimization points to the prevalence of a combination of factors, including poverty, lack of education, low socioeconomic status, low social mobility, limited employment opportunities, marginalization, corruption, conflict, weak governance and discrimination. Low self-esteem, domestic violence and addiction are also contributing factors. Comparative studies of vulnerability provide insight into the interconnectedness of factors and their relevance in context. In their study of the Badi community of Nepal, for example, Stacy Pigg and Pike (2004) point to the lack of social mobility and overall persistence of class rigidity as underlying factors. Steve Parish (1996) emphasizes the role of the caste structure in Nepal and persistence of purity and hierarchy as social norms. In her study of Devadasis in India, Orchard (2007) emphasizes the role of cultural practice, religion, custom and family obligation. Heather Montgomery (2011) discusses how familial and cultural expectations, including filial obligation, contribute to vulnerability to child prostitution in Thailand. In her study of the Dominican Republic, Denise Brennan underscores poverty and low social mobility as underlying factors (2004). Collectively, these studies emphasize the importance of addressing underlying factors contributing to vulnerability. They also provide ethnographic evidence that victimization is not one-size-fits-all and not evenly shared within each community, suggesting that a more complex dynamic underlies vulnerability and risk of victimization. Understanding this dynamic may help shed light on why prevention and protection remain such a challenge but also help guide anti-trafficking efforts and policies.

This paper contemplates the role of social exclusion and marginalization as factors contributing to vulnerability to human trafficking and risk of victimization. The focus is on the Roma population in Serbia, a socially excluded and marginalized group. The themes running through this inquiry address questions about whether: (1) members of the Roma population are vulnerable to human trafficking and have greater risk of victimization than non-Roma members in Serbia; (2) specific segments of the Roma population in Serbia (e.g., young, uneducated, displaced, women) are vulnerable to specific forms of human trafficking (e.g., forced begging, arranged/forced marriage) and have a disproportionately higher risk of victimization for these forms; (3) structural/formal and informal mechanisms contribute to vulnerability and risk of victimization. The authors suggest a sharper focus on underlying conditions and contextual factors would be helpful for improving prevention and protection and developing anti-trafficking strategies and policies in context-specific, gender-sensitive ways.

Part I: Patterns of Human Trafficking in Serbia

The evolution of human trafficking in Serbia mirrors the evolution of human trafficking in the larger context of globalization. The processes and consequences of globalization, including the loosening of some borders and tightening of others, rise in influence of non-state actors, rise in internal conflict and increase in demand for cheap labour, have contributed to and helped shape patterns of human trafficking. Serbia provides an interesting case given that the country has undergone multiple periods of transition as a result of conflict associated with the breakup in the 1990s of the Federal Republic of Yugoslavia (FR Yugoslavia) and linkage between conflict and human trafficking has been established. In *Baracks and Brothels*, for example, Sarah Mendelson (2005) highlights the ways the conflict in former Yugoslavia served as fertile breeding ground for human trafficking and calls attention to vulnerability during peacekeeping periods. A review of recent history in Serbia reveals shifting patterns of human trafficking in the *pre-conflict*, *conflict* and *post-conflict* periods, with notable shifts in activity during the conflict and post-conflict period. For this discussion, the *pre-conflict* period spans the mid-1980s to late 1980s; the *conflict* period covers the 1990s; the *post-conflict* period includes from 2000 through today.[3] Since Serbia was part of FR Yugoslavia (in some form) during most of this period up until 2006,[4] the discussion of patterns of human trafficking in Serbia incorporates cases from the FR Yugoslavia period that do not relate strictly to Serbia per se.

As is consistent with most national governments, data on human trafficking was not collected in a formal way in Serbia until 2002. In fact, human trafficking was first codified as a crime in Serbia in 2003. Despite the rather brief period for data collection, evidence of human trafficking victims from the region can be traced to late 1985 and 1986, as seen in cases involving forced prostitution, slavery and street begging of mostly Roma children (Djurić 1986, Pedrick 1986). In a 1985 case, Neso Djurić (1986) reported the arrest of 13 Yugoslavs by Austrian and Italian police for smuggling Roma children between the ages of 8 and 15 for 'prostitution, slavery or to be street beggars' and pointed to estimate suggesting 10,000 children from FR Yugoslavia were sold to Italian thieves from the period of 1975 onward. Djurić (1986) included an official statement indicating: '652 Yugoslav children, living without families, often victims of exploitation, begging and even committing crimes, were escorted to the border'. He reported that some children were purposely mutilated to get more in begging, referencing a social worker as stating: 'those who smuggle and own these children, mutilate them to draw pity when they place these deformed children into the streets to beg' (Djurić 1986). While data on the number of Roma children from FR Yugoslavia exploited for forced begging is elusive, the 1985 case (reported in 1986) highlights what might be referred to as *de facto* human trafficking victimization among Roma children during the mid-1980s. The 1986 case of 'Yugoslav Gypsies' also underscores this (Pedrick 1986). In this case, Clare Pedrick reported a 'child slave racket' where Roma children were used for begging, stealing and pick pocketing. According to Pedrick, Italian police identified 300 cases involving Roma children from Macedonia and Kosovo forced to engage in criminal behavior for organized criminal groups. The article referenced the case of 'a Gypsy who sold his own son in order to buy another child, one more adept at stealing' (Pedrick 1986). While human trafficking was not identified or codified as such at the time, the 1985 and 1986 cases suggest a possible *pre-conflict* pattern of human trafficking during the mid to late 1980s with FR Yugoslavia serving as a country of origin. The cases also represent threads of potential patterns of victimization of Roma children during the pre-conflict period. The extent to which Roma children were *disproportionately* vulnerable during this period is difficult to answer given the lack of systematic data. At minimum, the 1985 and 1986 cases point to vulnerability among Roma children for exploitation in forced labour conditions, such as forced begging, stealing and pick pocketing, and suggest *de facto* human trafficking victimization. Whether this was disproportionate at the time would depend on data on other victims, including non-Roma children in similar conditions.

While pre-conflict indications of human trafficking victimization are seemingly apparent, the conflict period is regarded less tentatively. During the period leading into the 1990s, as countries in Eastern and Central Europe experienced political and economic transition, shifts in patterns of human trafficking emerged in FR Yugoslavia. These shifts are closely connected with instability in the region and the strategic location of FR Yugoslavia between East and West, making it an ideal place to bring human trafficking victims from neighbouring countries. Whereas the 1985 and 1986 cases reflect labour trafficking of domestic victims (Roma), human trafficking in the form of commercial sexual exploitation became especially prominent during the conflict years and times of sanction in Serbia. During the 1990s, Serbia was a place of transit and destination for sex trafficking of foreign nationals. The combination of chaos, political and economic uncertainty, weak governance and a booming market in illicit goods made Serbia and other parts of FR Yugoslavia particularly attractive for human traffickers. At the time, the Balkans became known as a hot spot for human trafficking, earning it space among the six models of global human identified by Louise Shelley, i.e., 'Violent Entrepreneur Model: Balkan Crime Groups' (2003).

From a regional perspective, the loosening of borders in countries neighbouring FR Yugoslavia made it ideal for trafficking women from Eastern Europe to Western Europe. Furthermore, high levels of chaos and criminality confounding Serbia, Croatia and Bosnia and Herzegovina made for an interesting alliance among criminal networks (Andreas 2004). During this period, women from Romania, Moldova and Ukraine were brought to Serbia and forced to work in the commercial sex industry; others were later taken to countries in Western Europe (Shelley 2003). While the prevalence and scope of human trafficking in FR Yugoslavia during the conflict years is difficult to estimate, it is anticipated victims of sex trafficking were significant during the conflict years. Mendelson provides insight into the prevalence of sex trafficking during the conflict years and underscores the link between sex trafficking and demand for sex among international police and peacekeeping forces:

> When one US Special Forces officer was asked if he would have considered sharing information about human trafficking with the International Police Task Force (IPTF), he replied, 'Oh, they know. I would say ... they were the best customers. It was just common [...] knowledge [...]. You knew which houses were the brothels

and it was pretty common to see an IPTF or someone else in the U.N. community'
at these places. (Mendelson 2005)

Given the climate of weak governance during the conflict period, it is difficult to
determine with accuracy the scope of victimization and prevalence of foreign versus
domestic victims during the conflict years. It is also difficult to determine the extent
to which commercial sexual exploitation occurred alongside other forms, e.g., forced
begging, arranged/forced marriage. Furthermore, since human trafficking was not
codified as a crime in Serbia until 2003, and since awareness of human trafficking
was quite low, cases of human trafficking, particularly commercial sexual exploitation, were not recorded as such. Nonetheless, foreign victims were noted during the
conflict years.

The post-conflict period suggests a potential shift in patterns of victimization, the
hint of which is given in the shift in victims receiving assistance. According to
analysis of Safe House, ASTRA, Victimology Society of Serbia (VDS) and other anti-
trafficking organizations in Serbia, there is indication of a decline in foreign victims
and increase in domestic victims as seen by the drop in foreign victims receiving
assistance from 2003 onward and corresponding increase of domestic victims, with
domestic victims receiving assistance for the very first time in 2004 (Nikolić-
Ristanović *et al.* 2004, ASTRA 2010, Poucki 2012). While these indications are
striking, potential discrepancies between actual victims and victims receiving
assistance present a challenge for assessing shifts in victimization or vulnerability.
In Serbia and most European countries, there are additional challenges related to
privacy in data collection, making it difficult to glean from official data in Serbia the
extent to which Roma are vulnerable to human trafficking or experience a higher risk
of victimization.

Part II: Vulnerability among the Roma Population in Serbia

According to official census data, the Roma population represents the second largest
national minority group in Serbia.[5] The total population of Serbia is estimated to be
7.2 million (Statistical Office of the Republic of Serbia 2012). With 147,604 people
declaring as Roma in 2011, official estimates place Roma at just over 2 per cent of the
population. Unofficial estimates suggest a higher percentage at about 5 per cent,
taking into consideration not all Roma obtain identification cards, register with the
state or identify as Roma.

The Roma population in Serbia is a socially excluded, marginalized group. Roma
in Serbia experience some of the lowest levels of social mobility, economic activity
and education (UNICEF 2005, 2007, The Strategy for Improvement 2010). Estimates
suggest only about 27 per cent of the Roma population in Serbia are economically
active, placing the unemployment rate at four times that of the general population
(The Strategy for Improvement 2010). The poverty level among the Serbian
population is 6 per cent as compared to about 60 per cent among the Roma
population. Roma members are also least likely to obtain positions of authority

(The Strategy for Improvement 2010). Social exclusion, marginalization, prejudice and discrimination affect the life chances of Roma; they experience human rights violations with little recourse. Structural/formal and informal mechanisms, including stereotypes and prejudice, reinforce a generalized apathy with respect to the inequalities and injustice Roma experience.

In recognition of the harmful effects of systematic social exclusion and marginalization, The Decade of Roma Inclusion (2005–2015; hereinafter The Decade) was established as part of a larger European effort to address challenges affecting Roma in Europe, including in Serbia. The Decade is an international initiative of 12 member states and a variety of international partner organizations, non-governmental organizations, Roma and other civil society activists and donors. It was established in Bulgaria in 2005 in follow up to a conference in 2003 focused on Roma in the future of Europe.[6] The Decade's goal is to eliminate discrimination and close the gap between Roma and non-Roma in the societies in which they live. The Decade can be seen as an outgrowth of recognition from the United Nations (UN) and European Union (EU) of the need to address anti-Roma discrimination as a matter of critical importance for an expanding EU. Injustice, discrimination and human rights violations experienced by Roma represent a challenge to the security and stability of Europe and the larger international community, including the USA. The establishment of The Decade as a mechanism/framework to improve the situation of Roma reflects support for the UN Millennium Development Goals and its initiatives. The principles of anti-discrimination and equality expressed in the Copenhagen Criteria required for EU candidacy make the protection of Roma in Europe, especially in new or aspiring EU candidate countries, essential. While comprehensive analysis of The Decade and its impact is beyond this inquiry, especially since human trafficking victimization is not directly mentioned, The Decade has succeeded in raising awareness of processes of exclusion and marginalization of Roma and the consequences of those processes, including disproportionate vulnerability and victimization. Though not its intention, vulnerability and risk of human trafficking victimization among Roma have become part of this discussion.

The underlying conditions that contribute to vulnerability to human trafficking among the Roma population in Serbia include low social integration, low social mobility, poverty, stigmatization and stereotyping, overt and covert discrimination (e.g., from school authorities, teachers, school staff, other children), lack of documentation, language barriers, high number of internally displaced people from Kosovo, frequent change of residence or lack of official residence, lack of job opportunities, patriarchal culture, traditional lack of interest for schooling, especially among females, higher tendency for child labour due to the need for children to contribute to family income, etc. Some of these conditions, however, are also present among non-Roma members of Serbian society, which raises the question of the extent to which the Roma population or particular segments of the Roma population may be disproportionately vulnerable to particular forms of human trafficking.

Related questions involve the extent to which risk of victimization is disproportionate as well as the extent to which victimization of the Roma population would go unnoticed – particularly given the perception of Roma in Serbian society as 'other'.

In his pivotal work on human trafficking, Siddharth Kara stresses the need to identify not only the scale of human trafficking, but also more specifically which forms are prevalent in which contexts (Kara 2009). Despite difficulties associated with data collection, in recent years the Serbian government has improved its data collection and reporting mechanisms. Table 1 shows the overall distribution of forms of trafficking in Serbia in 2008 and Table 2 shows the distribution in 2012 for comparison purposes.

According to the data collected, sex trafficking is the leading form of human trafficking in Serbia, with forced begging as the second highest form. It is important to remember, however, that data collected is not the same as actual incidence, especially given difficulty of detection and identification. In analysing these numbers, it is particularly alarming that all victims of forced begging are underage children. While the tables do not reveal ethnicity or national identity due to privacy, underage victims are disproportionately of Roma background. In its study of underage victims from 2002 to 2003, VDS reports children of Roma background are disproportionately represented among the victims as compared to non-Roma children[7] (Nikolić-Ristanović et al. 2004: 103). The VDS report on male victims of human trafficking from 2003 to 2007 also identifies Roma children at disproportionately greater risk. In this study, of the 22 victims identified as domestic minors, 16 were of Roma background[8] (Nikolić-Ristanović 2009: 79–80). Furthermore, the US Department of State's TIP report from 2009 (the period following the VDS study) indicates that in Serbia: '[c]hildren, mostly Roma, continued to be trafficked for the purpose of sexual exploitation, forced marriage, or forced street begging' (2009). Though more data on Roma children trafficked for forced begging is needed, non-governmental organizations, law enforcement, Roma advocates and the US Department of State indicate that children of Roma background in particular are at risk for this form of human

Table 1 Distribution of human trafficking forms in Serbia for 2008.

| | Age and gender | | | |
| | Male | Female | | |
Trafficking forms 2008	Underage	Underage	Adults	Total
Sex		6	30	36
Forced begging	8	3		11
Forced labour		1	2	3
Force theft	1	1	1	3
Forced marriage		2		2
Total	9	13	33	55

Note: Data from Interior Ministry of Republic of Serbia (2008). Underage refers to below 18 years of age.

49

Table 2 Distribution of human trafficking forms in Serbia for 2012.

	Age and gender				
	Male		Female		
Trafficking forms 2012	Underage	Adults	Underage	Adults	Total
Sex		2	12	28	42
Forced begging	6		7		13
Forced labour		1		1	2
Force theft	3	1			4
Forced marriage			1	1	2
No exploitation took place			2	1	3
Total	9	4	22	31	66

Note: Data from Interior Ministry of Republic of Serbia (2012). Underage refers to below 18 years of age.

trafficking. In interviews with law enforcement, members of non-governmental organizations and Roma advocates, all confirm that Roma children are at risk for human trafficking, and are specifically vulnerable to sexual exploitation, forced prostitution, forced labour, forced begging, petty crime and arranged/forced marriage (Poucki 2012).

In reality, while a casual observer in Serbia is likely to observe Roma children begging, the linkage between this practice and human trafficking is only recently being made. The potential linkage between begging among Roma children and human trafficking raises questions about the extent to which Roma children engaged in begging are victims of human trafficking and how this functions in the larger picture of human trafficking in Serbia. An additional question is whether Roma children are disproportionately vulnerable to victimization via other forms of human trafficking, and moreover, whether structural/formal and informal mechanisms, including a combination of institutionalized anti-Roma discrimination, social exclusion, marginalization, bias and prejudice create the conditions for Roma children to become victims of human trafficking in Serbia. Perceptions of cultural practices, customs and traditions as well as other informal mechanisms are also relevant.

While research on the Roma population in relation to human trafficking is spotty, since the launch of The Decade of Roma Inclusion in 2005, more has been done. As early as 2004, VDS reported on a connection between Roma children, familial practices and human trafficking in Serbia: 'Roma children are most often sold by their parents who see this as a solution for their problems' (Nikolić-Ristanović et al. 2004: 119). This 2004 VDS study points to a case of a Roma girl trafficked by her family for begging and forced marriage. In general, begging and forced marriage are less explored in comparison to sexual exploitation. Nonetheless, VDS and other non-governmental organization (NGO) identify both as having particular relevance for the Roma population. Begging is largely regarded as compulsory or forced in Serbia and therefore a concern for practitioners working on anti-trafficking efforts. Reporting on a study conducted among anti-trafficking practitioners, including police, judges, non-governmental activists, social workers, etc., VDS points out:

> The majority of respondents believe that begging is well organized and that there is only a small number of true beggars who beg for themselves. The beggars are mainly divided according to the territory and they fight for it [...] Women and children mostly go to 'strategic' places – the busiest ones, where the fluctuation of people is largest. (Nikolić-Ristanović *et al.* 2004: 103)

Ethnographic research within the Roma community shows some acceptance of the idea that children should engage in labour and help with family income (Savić 2002, Mitro 2004). According to an interview with a Roma teacher in Novi Sad, this is often given as a reason Roma children do not attend school regularly, leave school early or drop out (Poucki 2012). In formal and informal capacities, the tendency for Roma children to work and the fact that this represents a violation of child labour laws and protection of human rights is often overlooked. From the perspective of child labour, there are two issues to consider. The first issue is that children under the age of 15 are working. The second is the conditions of their work. In many instances, their work requires them to be on the street and exposed to dangerous conditions, potentially representing a threat to their safety and worst form of child labour under the International Labour Organization (ILO 2010). This issue was underscored in the 2009 US Country Reports on Human Rights and Practices in Serbia:

> In urban areas, children worked in the informal sector as street vendors and car washers. In villages and farming communities, underage children commonly worked in family businesses. Children, particularly Roma, also worked in a variety of unofficial retail jobs, typically washing car windows or selling small items such as newspapers. Families often forced Roma children into manual labour and begging or trafficked them abroad to work in begging or theft rings. (US Department of State 2009)

The potential link between child labour and human trafficking among Roma is difficult to ignore, especially considering the tendency for Roma children to be involved in forced begging. Despite evidence that Roma children are forced to engage in labour under hazardous conditions, the severity of this issue is often disregarded due to lack of research and insufficient data on the number of Roma children engaged in forced labour effectively making them unnoticed or ignored. Systematic social exclusion and marginalization combined with abject poverty may create the conditions under which some Roma families support children begging. More research is needed, however, to map the role of structural/formal and informal mechanisms and external and internal incentive structures. To deny that some Roma children and families partake in decision-making is to deny agency; the authors seek to avoid that by suggesting more research is needed to understand push and pull factors. A further, and perhaps more pressing question, involves the extent to which activities such as begging are part of organized crime or just ad hoc survival modes.

The level of involvement of organized criminal networks in benefiting from forced labour of Roma children is unclear.

An interview with a young Roma boy reported in 2010 in Blic, a Serbian newspaper, provides some indication that the practice of Roma children begging is not only well organized, but often connected with beatings and physical abuse. The young Roma boy stated:

> I used to live with a friend whose father abused me and made me beg. He has a total of seven children of his own and he takes them all to beg. He tortures the oldest, who's seven, the most. Until recently he didn't want to buy him sneakers so he was begging barefoot. The four-year-old is also forced to stand in the streets for hours at a temperature of over 30 degrees Celsius. Each kid has to bring at least EUR 10, at the end of the day. If they bring less money, they get beaten. That's how it is with everybody. Older brothers sometimes control us, but usually everybody brings as much they should, because after so much beating nobody thinks about cheating. (Šević 2010)

This interview reveals the complexity of the situations in which Roma children find themselves. The interview discloses elements of organized crime, forced labour, familial abuse and exploitation. The young boy also describes how the territory/city of Belgrade is divided among criminal networks and how this limits him from begging in areas belonging to other bosses:

> They tell us where we're allowed to be. Each boss has his own territory where children work for him. Police used to chase us away from this intersection, but they usually just pass by. Still, as soon as we see them we run away. (Šević 2010)

This interview provides an example of the exploitation of Roma children through forced labour for financial gain. It can be treated as a potential indication of human trafficking *prima facie*.

Clearly, even without the cases described above, key indicators of risk for human trafficking are present among the Roma population. These indicators include poverty, lack of education, social exclusion, marginalization and low levels of upwards mobility, among others. What makes matters worse is the perception, appearance or social script that suggests giving, selling or renting of Roma children is somehow acceptable for Roma families and a normal part of Roma culture. From the gaze of the outsider (or insider looking out), it might be thought: if this is how they treat their own children, why should Serbian society or the government intervene? Of course, culture is complex and deeply nuanced; it might be that some practices and patterns are scripted, normalized or accepted among some members of the Roma and non-Roma population under certain conditions, yet that does not mean Serbian society, the government and members of the Roma population should ignore the call to address underlying conditions, improve prevention and protection strategies and develop viable alternatives. Indeed, in recent years, Roma advocates have begun to challenge structural/formal and informal mechanisms that allow such practices to continue with impunity.

While the cases described above may count as instances of human trafficking, especially those involving selling and renting children for forced begging, it is important not to cast artificially all cases of Roma children begging as human trafficking. Such assessments would need to be made on a case-by-case basis, which itself raises an important resource challenge. In Serbian society, given competing priorities and demands, motivating government officials to address the vulnerability of Roma children and their risk of human trafficking victimization, especially forced begging and arranged/forced marriage, requires sustainable efforts. The Decade's focus on Roma improvement coupled with Serbia's new status as EU Candidate may spur this along, especially considering the need for consistent EU policy on protection of national minorities and human rights and recent attention to trafficking of Roma children in Europe. A Europol report from 2011, for example, recognizes as a problem in Europe: 'trafficking of children by Roma criminal groups for exploitation in petty crime, and adults for the commission of benefit fraud'. This is also confirmed in the 2011 European Roma Rights Centre (ERRC) report, which provides alarming estimates of Roma victims (ERRC 2011). The ERRC report indicates: 'trafficking in persons affects Roma disproportionately'. Roma represents '50–80% of trafficked persons in Bulgaria, up to 70% in parts of the Czech Republic, at least 40% in Hungary, around 50% in Romania and at least 60% in Slovakia' (ERRC 2011: 11).

The findings from the ERRC report are staggering and prompt the need for better understanding about why members of the Roma population face a disproportionate risk. The ERRC report indicates that it did not find links between Roma cultural practices and other unique factors linking the Roma population to human trafficking. Rather, it identifies conditions placing the Roma population in a vulnerable position for human trafficking, including: 'structural forms of ethnic and gender discrimination, poverty and social exclusion which result in low educational achievement, high levels of unemployment, usury, growing up in state care, domestic violence affecting predominantly women and children and substance abuse' (2011: 11). The report also recognizes the role of family members in trafficking. Deeper analysis on the role of social exclusion and marginalization as well as the extent to which *normalization* of child labour as cultural practices, customs and traditions functions to allow these practices to continue uncontested. Such an understanding is critical for a more nuanced approach to effective prevention and protection and viable alternatives for sustainable livelihood. Responsible intervention among marginalized, vulnerable populations requires serious attention (Bain *et al.* 2013).

Raising the question of whether cultural practices, customs and traditions are linked to vulnerability is not to suggest Roma culture is to blame for any disproportionate risk of victimization, but rather to question whether certain aspects of cultural practices, customs and traditions and how they are *perceived* play a role in sustaining apathy (even contempt) and limiting political will to address the vulnerability of Roma, especially children. The perception that human trafficking is entangled in Roma customs, for example, may serve to not only undermine the human rights of

Roma victims but also allow an easy justification for this is a lesser priority. In an interview with a Roma advocate, the topic of culture was discussed:

> There is absolutely a link between culture and human trafficking among the Roma – it is just not spoken about. We have a very patriarchal culture. Women and children have to listen to men. If girls are told to marry someone, there is no choice. If girls are told not to go to school, there is no choice. Culture is a part of this. (Poucki 2012)

While culture may play a role, it is important to understand *the way* culture plays a role, including how cultural pressures from within and outside shape begging as a survival mechanism. A young Roma boy from Novi Sad explained the situation in simple terms:

> When I come home, I ask my mom if there is anything to eat. If she says we have 'beans', that means I don't have to go out and beg. If she says 'no', then I know I have to go out and beg. (Poucki 2012)

The issues facing Roma children are daunting and require political leadership as well as community support and cultural transformation. Through analysis of interviews with law enforcement and members of the Interior Ministry in Serbia, two themes are apparent: (1) they are aware of the risk of human trafficking for Roma children and (2) a coordinated plan for how to minimize these risks is elusive (Poucki 2012). The following excerpt from an interview with law enforcement in Novi Sad illustrates this: 'we can pick up all Roma kids from the streets in a day or two, but what do we do with them after that is an open question' (Poucki 2012). Awareness is clearly not enough; prevention and protection require a nuanced approach but also require viable alternatives. An interview with an NGO representative reveals:

> With children victims of trafficking, the situation is even worse. There is an unwritten rule that children victims have to be assisted by centres for social work. However, they do not have the capacities or knowledge to deal with such young victims. Moreover, in many instances they call us for help and directions regarding such cases. The last few cases we had confirm this exactly, since police and social centres just did not know what to do with them or where to go […]. Furthermore, when we talk about their help, we cannot speak about some meaningful psychological or therapeutic work with such children but rather only the provision of basic human needs, such as: shower, shelter and food. There is nothing more than that, even on our side. The NGO sector does not have the capacity or programs for more meaningful help for children. (Poucki 2012)

Vulnerability and disproportionate risk to children in Serbia, especially Roma children, is discussed in a 2011 report entitled 'Child Begging in Vojvodina', which provides data showing Roma children as most exposed to risk of begging and forced labour enforced by organized criminal groups (Muškinja Hajnrih *et al.* 2011: 18). The report also indicates that even when assistance is available for children, parents sometimes object to this, as provided in the excerpt below:

> [s]ome parents come to their shelter and request from them to forbid their child to come to the shelter since then they are not working for the family on the streets.

Furthermore, the same source claims that there are at least 90% of children under risk and exploited, mostly by their families. (Muškinja Hajnrih *et al.* 2011: 21)

The vulnerability and victimization that Roma children experience is part of a larger context of exclusion and marginalization in Serbia and Europe; as data becomes available, it is difficult to ignore. The Serbian Agency for the Coordination of the Protection of Victims (Ministry of Labour and Social Policies) recorded 127 trafficking victims in 2009. According to 2009 US Country Reports on Human Rights and Practices: 'Less than half of identified trafficking victims were children, mostly Roma, who were trafficked for the purpose of sexual exploitation, forced marriage, or forced street begging' (US Department of State 2009). This is consistent with findings in a report commissioned by the International Organization for Migration (IOM) in 2005 showing the Roma population as particularly vulnerable to human trafficking (Surtees 2005). 'Roma comprise a disproportionate share of assisted victims and (along with ethnic minorities generally) appear particularly vulnerable to trafficking in persons in Serbia' (Surtees 2005: 515). Similarly, representatives of ASTRA note a disproportionate level of vulnerability for Roma to become victims of human trafficking: 'after reviewing our data on a request of one Roma organization, we had found that it was something like a 50–50 ratio' (Poucki 2012). This pattern is not limited to Serbia, as observed in the ERRC report mentioned earlier as well as the IOM commissioned report revealing disproportionate risk for begging and sexual trafficking among Roma, especially in Bulgaria (Surtees 2005: 170, 187). A regional pattern of vulnerability and risk of victimization among the Roma population in Europe is difficult to ignore.

In many ways, efforts to incorporate Roma more fully into the larger society and revise structural/formal and informal practices that maintain isolation, exclusion and marginalization seem integral to a responsible strategy for prevention and protection of Roma in Serbia and throughout Europe. Given the impact of exclusion and marginalization in nearly all aspects of life, including education, socialization, housing and labour, it is both prudent and timely to develop and implement viable alternatives for sustainable livelihood and overcome obstacles to inclusion in education, society, housing and jobs. Ideally, such efforts would help create long-term solutions with a focus on the needs of Roma children. Further research on the role of normalization and in-group and out-group perceptions is critical for this endeavour as is the relationship between individual and collective identity.

Conclusion

Efforts to combat human trafficking in Serbia have grown over the years. Despite progress, significant challenges remain. Integrated strategies to combat human trafficking have not taken shape. A more dedicated focus on human trafficking victimization and minimizing vulnerability among the Roma population requires resources, training and political will. Such an effort would likely compete for support among other challenges facing Serbia, including political and socioeconomic instability. Additional concerns associated with collecting and analysing data, including ethical concerns over privacy and profiling, add another layer of complexity. Identification of culturally appropriate strategies for addressing vulnerability and victimization among the Roma population is critical, but a viable way forward is not clear. Efforts to involve members of the Roma community at all levels of decision-making in a more inclusive, community-based approach to minimizing vulnerability and risk of victimization offer promise, but also face challenges that are not as easily navigated, including deep prejudice and bias, conflict and in-group tension.

This paper acknowledges that the Roma population in Serbia is not a monolithic group; the paper does not suggest that all members of the Roma population in Serbia are disproportionately vulnerable to all forms of human trafficking. The paper rather analyses the underlying conditions that may contribute to: (1) higher levels of vulnerability among the Roma population, especially vulnerability to forms of human trafficking involving children, e.g., forced begging; and (2) apathy for or resentment of efforts to address the vulnerability of the Roma population in ways that go beyond awareness campaigns and reach deeper into transforming structures and challenging cultural expectations and normalizations that sustain vulnerability and limit the real or perceived availability of viable alternatives.

This inquiry suggests the need for more research on the relationship between individual and collective identity as well as in-group and out-group dynamics and their role in influencing interactions within and between the Roma population and non-Roma population in Serbia. The inquiry suggests that while cultural expectations and normalizations may not *cause* victimization, they play a significant role in sustaining vulnerability. The paper emphasizes the importance of addressing cultural expectations and normalizations when designing policies and strategies to combat human trafficking. The paper also underscores the importance of policies that aim to both minimize vulnerability and maximize viable alternatives for sustainable livelihood. The authors underscore the need for more research on human trafficking and the relationship between social exclusion and marginalization, individual choice, individual and collective identity, and structural/formal and informal mechanisms that reinforce cultural expectations and normalizations, including internal codes of behaviour, social scripts and coping mechanisms that may contribute to a disproportionately greater level of vulnerability and risk for particular forms of human trafficking among particular segments society. Finally, this inquiry urges more attention within the growing body of research on human trafficking to questions of vulnerability and risk among the Roma population throughout Europe.

Notes

[1]   The United Nations Convention against Transnational Organized Crime and its supplementary Protocol to Prevent, Suppress and Punish Trafficking in Persons, especially women and children, is commonly referred to as 'the Palermo Protocol' for brevity. To access the document, please go to: http://www.unodc.org/unodc/treaties/CTOC/.

[2]   Increased attention to the needs of victims is evidenced in the call for more rigorous research on the development of interventions that prioritize benefits to victims and guard against potential harm, particularly in light of the introduction and exploration of technology-based interventions to combat human trafficking. To this end, the authors collaborated with a team of researchers on a briefing to the White House on this. See http://www.danah.org/papers/TechnologistsCSEC.pdf.

[3]   The recent conflicts of FR Yugoslavia in which Serbia took part include the following: 1991 in Slovenia; 1991 through 1995 in Croatia; 1992 through 1995 in Bosnia and Herzegovina; 1999 in Kosovo.

[4]   Serbia and Montenegro remained united until 2006; Kosovo declared independence in 2008.

[5]   According to official statistics, Hungarians make up the largest national minority.

[6]   See Decade in Brief at http://www.romadecade.org/about-the-decade-decade-in-brief#.

[7]   This report identified 94 victims who were underage during the period 2002–2003, out of which 40 victims were of foreign origin, 34 were Roma and 20 Serbian (non-Roma). The victims were mostly female with an unspecified number of male victims.

[8]   Interestingly, the same report identifies only two Roma male adult victims of human trafficking among 342 male adult victims.

Works Cited

Andreas, P., 2004. Criminalized legacies of war: the clandestine political economy of the Western Balkans. *Problems of post-communism*, 51 (3), 3–9.

ASTRA, 2010. *Human trafficking in the republic of Serbia: report for the period 2000–2010*. Belgrade: ASTRA.

Bain, C., *et al.*, 2013. *How to responsibly create technological interventions to address the domestic sex trafficking of minors* [online]. Available from: http://www.danah.org/papers/TechnologistsCSEC.pdf [Accessed 3 January 2014].

Brennan, D., 2004. Selling sex for visas: sex tourism as a stepping-stone to international migration. *In*: B. Ehrenreich and A.R. Hochschild, eds. *Global women: nannies, maids, and sex workers in the new economy*. New York, NY: Holt, Henry & Company, 154–168.

Decade of Roma, 2005–2015. *Terms of references* [online]. Bucharest. Available from: http://www.romadecade.org/cms/upload/file/9292_file1_terms-of-reference.pdf [Accessed 1 January 2014].

Djurić, N., 1986. Yugoslav citizens arrested for smuggling. *Ottawa Citizen*, 2 January, p. 23. Available from: http://news.google.com/newspapers?nid=2194&dat=19860102&id=Zb8yAAAAIBAJ&sjid=nO8FAAAAIBAJ&pg=1317,124674 [Accessed 1 January 2014].

European Roma Rights Centre (ERRC), 2011. *Breaking the silence: trafficking in Roma communities* [online]. Budapest, ERRC. Available from: http://www.errc.org/cms/upload/file/breaking-the-silence-19-march-2011.pdf [Accessed 1 January 2014].

Europol, 2011. *Knowledge product: trafficking in human beings in European Union* [online]. The Hague, Europol. Available from: https://www.europol.europa.eu/sites/default/files/publications/trafficking_in_human_beings_in_the_european_union_2011.pdf [Accessed 1 January 2014].

International Labour Organization (ILO), 2010. Accelerating action against child labour. *In: International labour conference, 99th session 2010, report I(B)*, 2–18 June 2010. Geneva: ILO.

Interior Ministry of Republic of Serbia, 2008. Serbian version only [online]. Available from: http://www.mup.gov.rs/cms_lat/sadrzaj.nsf/statistika-2012-lat.pdf [Accessed 3 February 2014].

Interior Ministry of Republic of Serbia, 2012. Serbian version only [online]. Available from: http://www.mup.gov.rs/cms/resursi.nsf/statistika-2012-lat.pdf [Accessed 3 February 2014].

Kamler, E., 2010. NGO narratives in the global public sphere. *The international journal of diversity in organizations, communities and nations*, 11 (2), 75–86.

Kara, S., 2009. *Sex trafficking: inside the business of modern slavery*. New York: Columbia University Press.

Latonero, M., *et al.*, 2011. *Human trafficking online: the role of social networking sites and online classifieds. Centre on communication leadership and policy: research series* [online]. Social Science Electronic Publishing (SSRN Electronic Journal). Available at: http://technologyand trafficking.usc.edu/report/ [Accessed 3 January 2014].

Limanowska, B. and Rosga, A.J., 2004. The bar raid as 'outcome space' of anti-trafficking initiatives in the Balkans. *In*: E. Dunn, D. Dor, C. Baillie and Y. Zheng, eds. *Traveling facts*. Berlin: Campus, 154–176.

Mendelson, S., 2005. *Barracks and brothels. Peacekeepers and human trafficking in the Balkans*. Washington, DC: CSIS Press.

Mitro, V., 2004. *The invisible one: human rights of Roma women in Vojvodina*. Novi Sad: Futura Publikacije.

Montgomery, H., 2011. *An introduction to childhood: anthropological perspectives on children's lives*. West Sussex: Wiley-Blackwell.

Muškinja Hajnrih, A., Dragin, A., and Duškov, M., 2011. *Child begging in Vojvodina* [online]. Novi Sad, Ombudsman Provincial and Save the Children. Available from: http://www.unicef.org/ceecis/media_6204.html [Accessed 1 January 2014].

Nikolić-Ristanović, V., *et al.*, 2004. *Trafficking in people in Serbia*. Belgrade: OSCE and Victimology Society of Serbia.

Nikolić-Ristanović, V., *et al.*, 2009. *Trafficking of men in Serbia*. Belgrade: Prometej, Victimology Society of Serbia.

Orchard, T., 2007. Girl, woman, lover, mother: towards a new understanding of child prostitution among young Devadasis in rural Karnataka, India. *Social science & medicine*, 64 (12), 2379–2390.

Parish, S., 1996. *Hierarchy and its discontents: culture and the politics of consciousness in caste society*. Philadelphia, PA: University of Pennsylvania Press.

Pedrick, C., 1986. Oliver Twist-style child slavery ring brings thousands of youngsters into Italy. *Ottawa Citizen*, 18 June, p. 19. Available from: http://news.google.com/newspapers?nid=2194&dat=19860618&id=sKQyAAAAIBAJ&sjid=m-8FAAAAIBAJ&pg=1271,3695958 [Accessed 1 January 2014].

Pigg, S. and Pike, L., 2004. Knowledge, attitudes, beliefs and practices: the social shadow of AIDS and STD prevention in Nepal. *In*: S. Srivastava, ed. *Studies on contemporary South Asia: sexual sites, seminal attitudes: sexualities, masculinities, and culture in South Asia*. New Delhi: Sage Publications India, 271–300.

Poucki, S., 2012. *The quest for root causes of human trafficking: a study on the experience of marginalized groups, with a focus on the republic of Serbia*. Thesis (PhD). Rutgers University Community Repository.

Savić, S., 2002. *Women of minority groups in Vojvodina, review from the point of view of the majority nation*. Novi Sad: CMK Informator.

Šević, N., 2010. *Ne smeju kući ako ne donesu 1.000 dinara od prosjačenja. Blic on line* [They can't go home if they don't bring 1,000 dinars from begging] [online]. Translated from Serbian by S. Poucki. Belgrade: Ringier Axel Springer. Available from: http://www.blic.rs/Vesti/Hronika/203814/Ne-smeju-kuci-ako-ne-donesu-1000-dinara-od-prosnje [Accessed 3 January 2014].

Shelley, L., 2003. Trafficking in women: business model approach. *Brown journal of world affairs*, X (I), 119–131.

Statistical Office of the Republic of Serbia, 2012. *Census of population, households and dwellings in the republic of Serbia. Book 1* [online]. Belgrade. Available from: http://popis2011.stat.rs/?page_id=1103&lang=en [Accessed 2 January 2014].

Strategy for Improvement of the Status of Roma in the Republic of Serbia, 2010. Belgrade, The Ministry of Human and Minority Rights. Available from: http://www.inkluzija.gov.rs/wp-content/uploads/2010/03/Strategija-EN-web-FINAL.pdf [Accessed 7 January 2014].

Surtees, R., 2005. *Second annual report on victims of human trafficking in South-Eastern Europe* [online]. Geneva, IOM. Available from: http://lastradainternational.org/lsidocs/494%20 iom_2005_second_annual_report_on_victims_of_trafficking_in_south_eastern_europe_200 5_22.pdf [Accessed 3 January 2014].

UNICEF, 2005. *Serbia multiple indicator cluster survey: monitoring the situation of children and women* [online]. Belgrade, UNICEF. Available from: http://www.childinfo.org/files/MICS3_S erbia_FinalReport_2005-06_Eng.pdf [Accessed 1 January 2014].

UNICEF, 2007. *Breaking the cycle of exclusion: Roma children in South-East Europe* [online]. Belgrade, UNICEF-Serbia. Available from: http://www.unicef.org/ceecis/070305-Subregio nal_Study_Roma_Children.pdf [Accessed 1 January 2014].

UNODC, 2004. *Convention on transnational organized crime and protocols thereto* [online]. New York, NY, United Nations. Available from: http://www.unodc.org/unodc/treaties/ CTOC/ [Accessed 1 January 2014].

UNODC, 2008. *An introduction to human trafficking: vulnerability, impact and action* [online]. New York, NY, United Nations. Available from: http://www.unodc.org/documents/human-trafficking/An_Introduction_to_Human_Trafficking_-_Background_Paper.pdf [Accessed 2 January 2014].

US Department of State, 2009. *Country reports on human rights practices – Serbia* [online]. Washington, DC, US Bureau of Democracy, Human Rights and Labour. Available from: http://www.state.gov/g/drl/rls/hrrpt/2009/eur/136056.htm [Accessed 2 January 2014].

US Department of State, 2012. *Trafficking in persons report. United States of America* [online]. US Government document. Available from: http://www.state.gov/j/tip/rls/tiprpt/2012/index.htm [Accessed 2 January].

Sex Trafficking and the Sex Trade Industry: The Processes and Experiences of Nepali Women

Shobha Hamal Gurung

Over the past decade, girls' trafficking and the sex trade industries have intensified in contemporary South Asian nations, particularly in Nepal, India, and Bangladesh. The sex trafficking of Nepali girls and women into Indian brothels has been widely discussed on both local and global levels. In this paper, I examine cases of Nepali girls and women who were trafficked and sold into Indian brothels and illustrate how trafficking of girls and women has occurred within the intersections of larger structural conditions and micro level factors. By using gender, intersectional, and globalization/transnational perspectives, I analyze the processes and conditions under which sex trafficking occurred and women were forced into prostitution. The paper draws on an earlier study, follow-up research, personal communications, and secondary data to explore why, how, and under what circumstances women are forced into prostitution; what factors make them vulnerable or susceptible to sex trafficking; and how do globalization and transnational practices, Nepal's political economy, women's roles and position in Nepali society, gender socialization and perception, gendered culture of oppression, and kin and ethnic relations contribute to the trafficking of Nepali into the Indian sex industry.

Sex trafficking has become one of the most widely discussed phenomena of the 21st century in both the journalistic and academic worlds. Within the academy, scholars from various fields have offered their interpretations and analysis on why and how the issue of sex trafficking has become a rampant feature of the global economy. While some scholars have focused on the structural conditions such as poverty, unemployment, wars and regional conflicts, as well as the unstable political economy of the nation-states as the leading factors in increasing the rate of sex trafficking, other scholars have focused on the roles and processes of globalization and global restructuring to examine this burgeoning phenomenon.

Shelley (2010: 37), one of the leading experts on transnational crime and terrorism, linked human trafficking with '[...] lack of employment opportunities, poverty, economic imbalances among regions of the world, corruption, decline of border controls, gender and ethnic discrimination, and political instability and conflict'. Gender and feminist scholars in particular have focused on the race-, ethnicity-, caste-, class-, gender-, and nationality-based inequalities and discriminations to examine why some groups of women are vulnerable to sex trafficking and forced prostitution (Enloe 1990; Farr 2005; Limoncelli 2009; Crawford 2010).

Over the past decade, girls' trafficking and the sex trade industries have intensified in contemporary South Asian nations. Within the South Asian region, sex trafficking of Nepali girls and women into Indian brothels has increased over the years. Sex trafficking of Nepali girls and women has accelerated and moved beyond the South Asian region. So, what are the prevailing factors of this rampant condition? Is it poverty and unemployment? Is it regional inequality or social inequality? Is it illiteracy? Is it gender discrimination? Is it Nepal's political crisis and instability? Is it capitalism or patriarchy? Or is it some aspect of globalization or transnationalism?

I seek to answer these questions by analyzing intersecting regional, national, global, social, and economic inequalities, including the gendered culture of oppression and multiple forms of gender-based discriminations in Nepal. By focusing on the narratives of Nepali women carpet weavers, I analyze the conditions, factors, and processes under which a Nepali woman is subjected to sex trafficking and sold into (primarily) Indian brothels. In order to fully capture the multi-level operated and multiple-layered factored nature and process of sex trafficking – and to contextualize women's vulnerability and susceptibility within – I use global, gender, and intersectional frameworks. Women's experiences are at the core of the analysis, and I use first-person voice to interpret their narratives.

This paper draws upon both primary and secondary data. The primary data include (1) fieldwork, which included surveying 100 girls and women who were actual or potential victims and survivors of sex trafficking and the sex trade, and then interviewing a subset of this group; (2) my follow-up visit to Maiti Nepal in 2008; (3) interviews and personal communications with Ms. Anuradha Koirala and Bishwo Khadka (founder and Executive Director of Maiti Nepal, respectively) in 2012 during the Human Trafficking Conference at Southern Utah University; and (4) secondary sources.

First, I begin the paper with a discussion on the patterns and trends of human and sex trafficking both in global and South Asian perspectives. Second, I address my research context and methodology. Then I discuss the extent of sex trafficking in Nepal. Finally, I analyze three women's narratives from gender and intersectional perspectives and illustrate that the sex trafficking of Nepali girls and women is rooted in both macro- and micro-level factors and intersecting inequalities.

Human and Sex Trafficking: Global and Gender Perspectives

Human trafficking – which involves illegal transportation, recruitment, selling, and buying of human beings – occurs primarily for the purpose of labor and sexual exploitation (Hamal Gurung 2008). Human and sex trafficking has become increasingly transnational and fluid in the globalized twenty-first century. The increasing global and dramatic growth of human trafficking is interrelated with the various dimensions of global restructuring and globalization. Global restructuring and the social, political, and economic globalization have fuelled migration and immigration process; women are the hardest hit by this process. The demand and desire for an urban employment in the informal sectors have attracted vulnerable women to the cities, increasing their chance of being trafficked. Human trafficking is one of the most pervasive and darkest aspects of globalization (Limoncelli 2009), which thrives with the global networks of illicit and criminal activities (Shelley 2010). Human trafficking involves 'coercion and deception' to bypass consent in order to expedite people from their homes and families to areas where they will be instantly suppressed by the estrangement of the situation (Shelley 2010: 108). Shelley (2010) also linked the growth of the sex industry with the demise of the Cold War and the rise of globalization. As she (2010: 37) asserts, '[...] trafficking has increased dramatically with globalization, the rise of illicit trade, and the end of the Cold War.'

Different studies estimate different numbers of annual trafficked people. For example, Limoncelli (2008: 3) estimated '500,000 to nearly four million' are trafficked annually. Bales *et al.* (2009) reported around 27 million people currently enslaved around the world. The International Labour Organization estimates, '[...] the minimum number of persons in forced labor, including sexual exploitation, as a result of trafficking at any given time is 2.5 million. Of these, 1.4 million are in Asia and the Pacific [...]' (UN.Gift.Org. 2007: 6). According to the US Department of State's (2011) 'Trafficking in Persons Report', the estimated number of trafficked people varies from 4 to 27 million. These differing estimations indicate the complexity and challenges in data collection of these invisible, illicit, and underground activities. Limoncelli (2009) noted these methodological challenges about human trafficking studies, including the failure to come to a single consensus to define trafficking.[1]

The global patterns of human trafficking suggest that women and children comprise the majority of those who are trafficked for the purpose of sweatshop labor, domestic servitude, bondage labor, and prostitution (Bales 2004; Bales *et al.* 2009; Kara 2010; Shelley 2010). Studies have documented that the actual and potential victims and survivors of human trafficking are tricked or deceived by false promises of jobs in urban cities; they are also abducted and smuggled across borders during the internal and international migration processes (Hamal Gurung 2008; Kara 2010; Shelley 2010). They are then forced and coerced to sell their labor or sex or both.

Gender and feminist scholars locate the sexual- and labor-based exploitation of girls and women in patriarchy, capitalism, and a series of other intersecting inequalities. While radical feminists blame patriarchy for women's sexual and labor exploitation, Marxist feminists locate the problem in colonialism, slavery, class formation, and capital expansion. Kamala Kempadoo (2004: 53) in *Sexing The Caribbean* reported that during the colonial invasion in the Caribbean, 'concubines served as both mistresses and housekeepers and were sometimes hired out by their owners to sexually service other men in order to obtain cash'. Enloe (1990) documented the growth of sex workers and the sex industry in South Korea with the militarization and the expansion of the US army-bases. Scholars have thus analyzed the roles of colonization, militarization, patriarchy, and capitalism in intensifying the commodification of women's labor and sexuality.

Intersectional feminist scholars take further steps in recognizing the race-, class-, caste-, ethnicity-, nationality-, citizenship-based inequalities and discriminations in relation to women's labor and sexual exploitation. Intersectional theory, which was introduced by Kimberle Crenshaw in 1989 and developed and analyzed by Patricia Hill Collins (1990) in *Black Feminist Thought*, recognizes and acknowledges multiple sources of exploitation and subordination. Intersectional scholars suggest that the intersections of race, class, and gender create a 'complex inequality' (McCall 2001) or a 'matrix of domination' (Collins 1990). Building on the feminist-based political economy approach, Limoncelli (2009: 265–266) called for a gendered political economy of trafficking framework that would

> [...] allow us to question the reasons for and consequences of markets that commercialize women's bodies and their labour and call attention to the ways racial/ethnic, class, and national inequalities are fuelling sex industries within and across countries.

From an intersectional framework, the increased sex trafficking and the sex trade of girls and women is rooted in their race-, ethnicity-, caste-, class-, nationality-, and citizenship-based positions and inequalities. Within a global and transnational framework, free markets, open borders, global capitalism, and transnational networks and practices contribute to human and sex trafficking. In upcoming sections, I use these frameworks to examine the processes of sex trafficking of Nepali women into Indian brothels.

Research Context and Methods

In the 1990s, while I was conducting my research on Nepali women carpet weavers, I became interested in exploring the issue of sex trafficking and the sex trade. During this time, the sex trafficking of Nepali girls and women to the brothels in India was gaining increasing attention. Frequently, I would read about cases of girls being trafficked into Indian cities where they were sold into the sex trade. Carpet factories were frequently cited as places through which girls and women were trafficked. I inquired about the relationship between carpet factories and sex trafficking with the management personnel of some carpet factories, as well as nongovernmental organizations (NGOs), social workers in the area, members of the local community, and the police. My conversations with these various groups of people confirmed a connection between the carpet factories and sex trafficking. It was in that context that I became interested in exploring the relationship between the work in the carpet factory and the sex trafficking of Nepali girls and women. I then approached and visited relevant NGOs through personal contacts and social networks. Some of the NGOs that I visited include Maiti Nepal, ABC/Nepal, the Women's Rehabilitation Centre, Children Workers in Nepal, and Santhi Purnasthapana Kendra. I also visited the Children and Women's cell of Kathmandu Valley Police Station in Hanuman Dhoka, Kathmandu.

The research participants in this study include women who were the victims/survivors of sex trafficking and sex trade or those intercepted by the NGOs and police en route to trafficking to Indian brothels.[2] By using snowball sampling, I selected research participates. I gathered socioeconomic and demographic information through surveys, interviews, and secondary sources on 100 girls and women (ranging in age from 14–40) who were victims and survivors of trafficking. Out of this group, I selected 10 girls and women from the ABC/Nepal and Maiti Nepal NGOs for focus group interviews and narrative analyses.[3]

The case studies that I present in this study are based on my focus group interviews and individual narrative collection with those girls and women who were trafficked and forced to become prostitutes in Mumbai, India. The focus group interviews and narrative collections took place in the transit homes of ABC/Nepal and Maiti Nepal, where the girls and women were rehabilitating at the time.[4]

I kept the interview questions semi-structured and open-ended so that the participants could narrate their stories with their own chains of thought. As I listened to their stories, I simultaneously took notes. The interviews were conducted in the Nepali language, which I later transcribed and translated. Again in 2008, I revisited Maiti Nepal and met with the staff members for follow-up interviews. In 2012, Mrs. Anuradha Koirala visited Southern Utah University to deliver a keynote address at a human trafficking conference, then again I had the opportunity for additional follow-up interviews and personal communication with her and her executive director. Through these discussions, I learned about the new trends and directions of sex trafficking in Nepal.

Human Trafficking: South Asia

South Asian nations, particularly India, Nepal, and Bangladesh, are hardest hit by sex trafficking and sex trade industries. Referring to the South Asian region, UN.Gift.Org.

reports, '[...] it is estimated that 150,000 victims are trafficked from the region annually. Many studies have revealed that trafficking in women and children is on the rise in Asia. Trafficking for commercial sexual exploitation is the most virulent form of trafficking in the region' (2008: 8). Despite the collaborative efforts of the local, national, and international community to prevent and combat sex trafficking and the sex trade, the rate of sex trafficking has increased dramatically in South Asia. Huda (2006: 375) reported that '[...] every year 1 to 2 million women, men, and children are trafficked worldwide, around 225,000 of them are from South Asia (India, Nepal, Pakistan, Bangladesh, Sri Lanka, Maldives, and Bhutan).'

Sex Trafficking in Nepal: Trends, Destinations, and Directions

The sex trafficking of Nepali girls and women has now become a rampant issue (Wilson 1997; Miller 2006; Hamal Gurung 2008). According to the US State Department's annual Trafficking in Persons report, Nepal is ranked as a Tier 2 source country (US Department of State 2011). According to Deane (2010: 494), about '7,000 Nepalese women and girls are trafficked for prostitution to the Asia Pacific area alone'. The ILO/IPEC (2002) reported around 12,000 Nepali girls are trafficked every year for sexual exploitation. Nepali NGOs reported between 5,000 and 7,000 girls and women are sold into Indian brothels each year (Ghimire 1994; Pradhan 1994). The *Times of India* reported around 100,000 Nepali sex workers in Indian brothels in 1989 (Ghimire 1997). Adhikari (2007) reported that there were around 200,000 Nepali girls working in the Indian brothels.

Although various NGOs, INGOs, media, and studies have provided estimated numbers/cases of sex trafficking, these numbers are only based on reported cases. Because sex trafficking is illicit trade and it manifests underground, the cases are difficult to detect or count. Actual cases of sex trafficking are, therefore, higher than the reported ones. As similar to the global patterns, the reported numbers of sex trafficking in Nepal are also inconsistent. There seems to be, however, a consensus that the majority of Nepali girls and women are trafficked into the Indian brothels. India is the hub of the sex industry in South Asia. It is the main destination and transit nation for many South Asian trafficked people, particularly Bangladeshi, Nepali, and Pakistani girls and women. Hynes and Raymond (2002: 199) stated, 'Brothels in Bombay and Delhi receive trafficked women from Bangladesh and Nepal and are often the transit point for moving women to Europe and North America'. Farr (2005) reported that in Mumbai alone there were approximately 60,000 Nepali sex workers. According to Hynes and Raymond (2002: 199), 'The trafficking of girls from Nepal to India is probably the most intensive sexual slave trade anywhere in the world'.

Although India has been the main destination for the trafficked Nepali girls and women, the recent trafficking patterns of Nepali women indicate its increasing global expansion. Now, Nepali women are trafficked through different routes and for various other destinations and nations. In particular, since the late 1990s and early

2000s, the flow and direction of trafficking has been to various Gulf nations and Southeast Asian nations (personal communication with Anuradha Koirala, 2012). While Nepali girls and women in Gulf nations are mainly used in the private sphere as domestic workers, in bordering Tibetan city in Khasa,[5] they are forced to become sex objects and entertainers in public spaces. According to the UNDP Asia-Pacific Regional Centre reported that (2009: 97) 'Hong Kong (SAR) is the second biggest market for trafficked Nepalese women; and Malaysia, the United Arab Emirates (UAE), and other Gulf countries are also reported to be destinations.'

Recently, an increasing number of Nepali girls have been trafficked to various cities in China where they are forced to work in 'cabin restaurants' and dance bars (personal communication with Anuradha Koirala, 2012). The daily newspaper, *MyRepublica* in Nepal reported '...there are six dance bars, 20 cabin restaurants, 10 hotels, and 20 lodges in operation in the red light area of Khasa and there are at least five women engaged in the flesh trade in each one of them.' The newspaper also indicated the open China-Nepal border policy as a contributing factor. Quoting Ms. Kopila Tamang, Supervisor at Santi Punarsthapana Griha, the author reported that, 'the flesh trade has boomed because of the free China-Nepal border policy. Many girls working in restaurants in Kathmandu and Pokhara end up in Khasa, lured by hopes of making more money,' said Tamang. (http://www.myrepublica.com/portal/index.php?action = news_details&news_id = 53822).

Actual Victims/Survivors and Potential Victims: Socioeconomic and Demographic Backgrounds

This study is based on an analysis of the lives of 100 girls and women who were actual victims/survivors or potential victims of sex trafficking and the sex trade.[6] Of the 100 girls and women, 78 per cent were actual victims/survivors and 22 per cent were potential victims of trafficking and the sex trade. The majority of the research participants in this study were relatively poor, young, unmarried, and less-educated migrant girls and women from the rural hills and mountain regions of Nepal.

A sharp regional inequality still persists in Nepal. Social and physical infrastructures are underdeveloped in many hill and mountainous regions of Nepal, which impact its human capital. Most people are illiterate or semiliterate, landless, submarginal, and poor peasants who exist at the bottom rungs of Nepalese society. Income-earning alternatives other than construction and agriculture-based work are often lacking in the region. The majority of girls and women in this study came from these particular geographical and socioeconomic backgrounds.

In terms of caste and ethnic components, slightly more than 50 per cent of the research participants belonged to Tibeto-Burman ethnic groups such as Tamang, Gurung, Rai, and Magar. The caste groups included Brahmin, Kshatriya, Newar, Tharu, and Dalit (Hamal Gurung 2003). Although previous studies (Ghimire 1994, 1997; Pradhan 1994; Kaufman and Crawford 2011) noted that most trafficked women originate from the ethnic minority community, my (2003) study illustrated that regional, socioeconomic, and gender-based inequalities factored more than caste and ethnic factor.

In terms of religion, Buddhism and Hinduism were the main religions of the majority of the women: 61 per cent were Hindu, 37 per cent were Buddhist, and the remaining 2 per cent were Christian or Muslim (Hamal Gurung 2003). In terms of age, the majority of the girls and women surveyed in the study were young, ranging from 14–20 years of age. Fifty eight per cent of the girls and women were unmarried. Information on the educational backgrounds of the girls and women indicated that the majority of them had never been to school (Hamal Gurung 2003).

Sex Trafficking and the Sex Trade: Between Multiple and Intersecting Inequalities

Scholars have offered various explanations about why Nepali girls and women are trafficked for the sex trade industry. Scholars have suggested (Huda 2006; Simkhada 2008) the structural-level conditions such as poverty, population growth, and urbanization as the root causes in the increasing growth of human/sex trafficking. Datta (2005) linked the increasing sex trafficking problem between Nepal and India with the open border between these two nations and free movement of people. In their study 'Research and Activism Review: Sex Trafficking in Nepal: A Review of Intervention and Prevention Programs', Kaufman and Crawford (2011: 652) also identified the multiple root causes of trafficking in Nepal, '[…] including poverty, the low status of women, and migration in an attempt to escape insurgent violence'. I argue that the dramatic increase in the sex trafficking of Nepali girls and women is rooted in multiple factors, multi-level inequalities, and the intersection of these inequalities. The factors vary from larger structural level inequality (i.e. regional and gender) to personal level violations of trust and love.

Feminist sociologists as well as race, class, and gender scholars have employed intersectional theoretical approaches to interpret the multiple marginalities and inequalities of their research subjects (Choo and Ferree 2010). For intersectional scholars, the effects of race, ethnicity, class, gender, sexuality, nationality, and citizenship status are experienced together, not separately. By employing the intersectional and global/transnational frameworks, I analyze women's lived experiences in upcoming sections. These narratives also represent the multiple and intersecting factors of other participants' sex trafficking process and their everyday lived reality.

The Geopolitical and the Political Economy of Nepal

Geopolitical relationships between Nepal and India and fluid open border policies as well as sexual and labor commodification of Nepali girls and women contribute to the extent of sex trafficking of Nepali girls into the Indian brothels. The main contributing factors include India being a neighbor in the east, west, and south of

Nepal; an open border; easier migration and immigration (no visa restriction to enter India and no work permit needed to work); and similarity of culture and language.

Nepal is a landlocked country; the majority of its international trading and business is still conducted through the Kolkata port in India. The Indo-Nepal trade and open border agreement was designed to facilitate trade and transit between Nepal and India. There is, however, no agreement regarding the movement of people and the routes they take (Deane 2010: 496). Unfortunately, the people who are involved in sex trafficking and the sex trade industry take advantage of such conditions. The geopolitical and sociocultural relations between Nepal and India thus provide favorable conditions for the traffickers and the pimps to transport and traffic Nepali girls and women.

Gender, Sexuality, and Gender Discrimination

While sex work can be a personal choice for some, it is forced upon many others (Hamal Gurung 2008). None of the girls and women in this study became sex workers by choice, but by trick, deception, and coercion. The gender- and sexuality-based sociocultural, economic, political, and legal discriminations, inequalities, and oppressions make some particular groups of women vulnerable for sex trafficking.

Historically, the labor and sexual oppression and exploitation of Nepali women occurred for various sociocultural and political reasons. For example, the 'Deuki' system in Nepal provided the rich aristocrats, feudal lords, and wealthy families with the option to buy young girls to offer to temple idols in the Hindu tradition to fulfill their wishes (Hamal Gurung 2008). These girls were forbidden to marry and were provided with no other means of support beyond contributions to the temple. Without having any other earning alternative for their livelihoods, these girls were then compelled to become prostitutes (Hamal Gurung 2008).

Similarly, girls and women in the 'Badi' community (the lowest caste in Nepal) traditionally earned their livelihood by singing and dancing (Hamal Gurung 2008). Due to economic factors, they were later pushed into prostitution (Hamal Gurung 2008). The historical commodification of women's labor and sexuality has now become a global epidemic. What exacerbates this condition is the perception and treatment of women as a saleable commodity whose sexual labor can be sold and resold in the global sex trade.

What makes a particular woman susceptible for sex trafficking is her spatial location, socioeconomic position, demographic backgrounds, roles and position in the family, and her personal life and interests (e.g. a conflicted married life, desire to work). These are often the marginalized group of women in the particular community and setting. The illicit networks of people then facilitate the sex trafficking process. The narratives that I present in the following sections illustrate the interrelationship and simultaneous operation of multi-level factors in the manifestation of sex trafficking.

Sold into Brothel: Processes and Experiences

From Gendered Migration to the Urban Employment

Out of the 100 girls and women in this study, 45 per cent were trafficked en route to their fictive work in Kathmandu or Mumbai. Some sex trafficking occurred within the migration process.[7] The majority of the traffickers were the women's acquaintances, friends, fellow villagers, or others whom the women trusted the most such as boyfriends and husbands.[8] A violation of love, trust, friendship, and kinship was prevalent in all cases. Based on the data collected from the 100 girls and women, 28 per cent of them were trafficked by a labor contractor or pimp, 19 per cent through the social circle of the carpet factories, 19 per cent through boyfriends or husbands, 18 per cent through fellow villagers, 7 per cent through male relatives and friends, 3 per cent through female relatives, and the rest through other contacts.

Assurances of work in a carpet factory or in an Indian city are the most common ploys used by traffickers to lure girls and women directly from their villages. Fake marriages and trips to a big Indian city are the most popular ploys used by traffickers to lure girls and women from carpet factories. In the case of those directly trafficked from their home villages, the traffickers included uncles; stepfathers; fellow villagers, both male and female; and the pimps and brokers of the brothels. In the case of those trafficked from carpet factories, the majority of the traffickers were a combination of boyfriend and pimp or broker. In other cases, the traffickers were a combination of fictive husband and pimp or broker. These fictive husbands marry only to sell their wives for a profit. Such was the case of Reeta, a 22-year-old brothel returnee, who was married just to be sold. In next section below, I present Reeta's story. She shared her story with me at ABC/Nepal's transit home in 2000.

Factory Work: Gender, Sexuality, and Sex Trafficking

The carpet factory is a microcosm of the young rural migrant population in Kathmandu. The majority of adolescents and teenage girls come to work in carpet manufacturing and live together with their friends, relatives, or fellow villagers to earn an income and experience modern city life. The availability of young and naïve rural girls makes carpet factories a locus for sex traffickers and brokers to 'recruit' girls and women. The questions then are: Who is vulnerable? What are the ways of trafficking?

Reeta was from the southern plains region of Nepal. She went to Kathmandu with her four friends to work in a carpet factory. Three of her friends had been working in the factory in Kathmandu for some time. Reeta and another friend from her village met their old friends when they had returned home for a festival. These friends told them about the modern city life and the cash they earned working in the carpet factory. They told them how much fun it was to watch movies, go to the circus, and do fun stuff. Reeta and her friend also noticed their nice clothes, shoes, watches, fancy hair clips, and make-up. Wanting to earn an income and experience the city life, Reeta and her friend decided to leave their village to accompany their friends to work in the carpet factory. Their friends assured them of jobs in the same carpet factory in Kathmandu if they came with them.

Upon arriving in Kathmandu, they began to work in one of the carpet factories in the Boudhanath area. During her work in the carpet factory, Reeta got to know a man through one of her friends. After a while, Reeta and this man started going out together to movies and the park. After a few months, the man proposed marriage to her. Reeta told him that she would talk to her parents and get their permission when she visited them during the next festival. She told him to wait until then. The man, however, kept trying to persuade her to get married soon. Living alone and unmarried or living together without marrying is still socially unacceptable in Nepali society. This puts lots of pressure for women to get married, especially if she is not educated and economically independent. Feeling pressured by the gender norms and the factory work culture, Reeta agreed to marry the man.

One day her new husband said that he would take her to see a big city in India – Mumbai. Since her arrival in Kathmandu, Reeta had been watching Bollywood movies, so she was very excited to go to Mumbai where these films are produced. On their way to Mumbai, they met up with a man who accompanied them the rest of the way. Her husband introduced him as his cousin. Upon arrival at a Mumbai train station, they stopped to get something to eat. Her husband went to buy cigarettes and did not return. Reeta later found out that her husband's 'friend' was in fact a pimp for one of the brothels in Kamathipura, the infamous red light district of Mumbai. Reeta's husband had sold her to this pimp, and the pimp sold her to a brothel, making additional profit. In a brothel in Kamathipura, Reeta was coerced into becoming a prostitute. She ended up working as a commercial sex worker in the brothel for three years.

As Reeta's case illustrates, sex trafficking occurs within a pre-planned scheme from trafficker's side. Various multilayered personal, micro, and macro factors provide an ideal stage for the pre-planned scheme to be successful. Initially, it might appear that Reeta's attempt to earn and make a living in Kathmandu city brought her into the sex trade. But Reeta's trafficking into the sex trade only proceeded successfully when multiple factors functioned together. An analysis of Reeta's case through an intersectional framework allows us to understand the interrelationship of these factors.

According to the intersectional framework, the issues of oppression, domination, exploitation, marginalization, and privilege are rooted not just in one single factor such as poverty but in various other factors such as race, class, gender, sexuality, nationality, and citizenship status. These factors intersect and operate simultaneously and create an interlocking system of oppression, exploitation, and privilege. The interlocking system of oppression and domination is also structured on several levels such as personal, community, and institutional (Collins 1990).

Multiple factors also manifested both locally and transnationally in a simultaneous fashion in Reeta's life. For instance, the entrenched gender ideologies, beliefs, and perceptions that drove her to marriage; a desire for a modern life; Reeta's demographic background (particularly her young age, minimal level of education, and marital status); and her naïveté had contributed to Reeta's trafficking into the sex trade industry.

Marriage and sexuality hold special places in the lives of Nepali girls. Daughters are expected to marry; their sexual relationship with a man is permitted only after marriage. Social, intimate, and sexual relationships between men and women without marriage are not acceptable in Nepali society. Although they were away from home and the factory work provided them with freedom of movement, the girls were still aware of the gender norms and beliefs.

They knew it was expected of them to get married. They knew if they explicitly intermingled with the boys or were involved with them sexually, they would be perceived as loose women. So, when Reeta started to date the man and when he proposed marriage, she agreed. Like any other married Nepali women, Reeta also fully trusted her so-called husband for all the decisions he made. She was excited to go to India; she never questioned his plans and decisions. Reeta was barely literate; she was from the rural hill area and lacked knowledge and experience of exploitive practices.

The man took full advantage of her innocence. He also benefitted from the patriarchal gendered culture (norms, beliefs), which granted social, economic, and political power and privilege to a husband. Reeta's geographic and socioeconomic locations, demographic background (including gender norms and beliefs), and gender roles and relations were sources of her condition. Marriage in Nepalese society is supposed to ensure a woman's protection and security, yet Reeta — who married for these things — was sold by her own husband.

From global and transnational perspectives, capitalist expansion, easy money, monetary gain, and profit motivated her fictive 'husband' to traffic Reeta. The sex trafficking process was mediated and facilitated by the geopolitics of India-Nepal, including the open border and free flow of people between Nepal and India and the transnational networks of people in both nations who are involved in the underground sex trade industry.

From Gendered Culture of Oppression to the Violation of Ethnic Relations

My previous study indicates that girls and women from certain family structures (such as those who come from broken homes, whose parents have died, who have blended families, who have been abandoned by their husbands, or who have general conflict and tension in their family) are desperate to get wage work in the cities. Patriarchal household relations and gendered culture of oppression intensify their familial experience. Women and girls from such family situations are easily convinced to leave their villages, whereupon they also become vulnerable for sex trafficking (Hamal Gurung 2003).

Tara, a 28-year-old woman, was from a poor peasant family in a hill region of Nepal. Her mother died when Tara was six years old and her father remarried. Tara's relations with her stepmother were never good. When Tara was eight years old, she was responsible for taking care of her siblings, collecting water and fodder, and taking care of the livestock. She was never sent to school. When she reached the age of 15, her stepmother arranged her marriage to a man in the same village. After her marriage, Tara was sent to live with her husband and his extended family. Her workload intensified after her marriage; she was responsible for all the household chores, including farm and livestock work. Every day, she cooked food and served it to all the family members, but was the last one to eat. Her daily work began at 4:30 a. m. and ended around 10:00 p.m. She barely had any time for herself or for her husband. In terms of social and economic position and power, she was at the bottom of the familial hierarchy. Although she was the main source of the household and farm labor, she did not have access to any resources and she did not have any decision-making power in the household.

When Tara was 18 years old, her husband left home in search of wage work in the city and never contacted her or returned home. Neither her parents nor her in-laws showed any affection toward or responsibility for Tara. She was seen as an abandoned wife and was often humiliated and embarrassed by her family and neighbors. Despite the oppressive family relations and exploitative work conditions, Tara continued to stay with her in-laws where she suffered alone and in silence.

One day, when she was returning from collecting fodder, she met a couple along the way. They were fellow villagers from her own ethnic community. They knew her situation and they expressed sympathy. They suggested that Tara should look for a job in India. They told her that their relatives worked in Delhi, India and that if she wanted, they could take her there and help her get a job. Given her shattered conjugal life, oppressive household relations, heavy workload, lonely and miserable life, and lack of economic resources, Tara decided to go with them. Tara did not have any caring and loving close family members or friends who could have mediated her decision to go to India. On her way to the fictive job in India, Tara was trafficked into the sex trade in Mumbai. Tara's fellow villagers were in fact local-level recruiters/traffickers who worked for Indian sex traffickers.

Nepal is a patriarchal, patrilineal, and patrifocal society; its norms and values are heavily patriarchal (Hamal Gurung 2003). 'The patriarchal social system contributes to unequal land and resource distribution, and unequal social, economic, and political power relations at both household and societal levels' (Hamal Gurung 2003: 243). Although gender roles and relations vary according to class, caste, ethnicity, education, religion, age, and marital status, uneducated, rural, and impoverished women tend to suffer particularly severe consequences of living in a strongly patriarchal household and society (Hamal Gurung 2003).

Tara's decision to leave her village and earn an income was due to her personal and familial life, her marginal economic situation, and the exploitative gendered division of labor, as well as the oppressive gender relations in her household. She was marginalized and oppressed at personal, community, and societal levels. Her father in her natal home and her father-in-law in her husband's home controlled the land and other economic resources. Tara didn't have any economic resources to support herself; she was fully dependent on her parents-in-law for food and shelter. Although she was the major source of the household and the farm work, she was not valued. Her suffering and oppression were invisible to others. It was within this context that she became vulnerable and a possible candidate for sex trafficking. Her fellow villagers, the local-level traffickers, knew her situation. They were looking around, using this type of information to identify young girls and women for sex trafficking.

Thus Tara was trafficked by her own fellow ethnic villagers. They betrayed her as a member of the same village, ethnic community, and nation. Tara trusted them because of their shared geographical location, ethnicity, gender (one of them was female), and nationality and the traffickers were able to transport her to India due to this trust. They took her to Mumbai and sold her to an Indian trafficker. Their shared culture and nationality also made the Indo-Nepal border crossing smooth and easy. The Indian trafficker, in turn, sold her into the sex trade.

From a transnational perspective, Tara's journey from her village to Kamathipura occurred through a series of local and transnational connections and practices. Profit-motivated actors at various levels from within and across the nations were operating in the underground and lucrative sex industry. Tara's traffickers initiated sex trafficking at the local level, they facilitated international border crossing, and they traded and supplied Tara for the international sex trade industry. One of the main tasks of local traffickers seems to be facilitating the illegal national and international border crossing (from Nepal to India).

Sex Trafficking: Among and Between Women

Meera, a 24-year-old woman, is from a farming family in the western hill region of Nepal. By her own choice, she came to Kathmandu with her sister and brother-in-law to work in a carpet factory when she was 15 years old. She had been attending a middle school back home and helping her parents in farm work. But she had wanted to see and live in the city. So when her sister and brother-in-law were leaving for Kathmandu, her parents let her go with them. After weaving carpet in the factory for about six months, she left the factory with a group of friends that she had made there. Together, they started to work in another carpet factory for more money. In the new factory, Meera met new people and made new friends.

Factory work culture permitted intermingling and interaction with the male workers. There was no gender restriction on freedom of movement. Having an affair and marrying a fellow worker featured in the factory work culture. Two of Meera's girlfriends had already married. Meera felt societal pressure to get married. She also felt that the boys were eyeing her body and that they were interested in her only for sexual reasons. She often encountered obscene remarks and teasing about her body and sexuality. She felt a need to get married and to be protected.

One day two men came to work in the factory. After a few weeks, two of their female relatives (*didis*) came to visit these new male workers. One day, while Meera was weaving carpet, one of the *didis* approached Meera and started asking about her personal life. She asked Meera what her dream was and how she wanted to live her life. Meera was fascinated with the modern city life and she liked watching Bollywood films. She shared her interest with the *didi*. The *didi* started to interact with Meera on a regular basis and gradually they became friends.

One day, the *didi* told Meera that a friend of hers worked in one of the Bollywood actors' houses in Mumbai where all the Indian movies are made. The *didi* also told Meera that her friend could easily find her a high-paying job in Mumbai. Meera was tired of weaving carpet and of factory work culture. Hence, she was tempted by the offer of a high-paying job. More than anything, she was excited about Bollywood movies and the glamour of Mumbai city life. She agreed to go to Mumbai with the two *didis* and they left the next week. Upon their arrival in Mumbai, they took a taxi and went to meet the *didi's* friend. Meera later found out that she was in a brothel house – the *didi's* friend was in fact a brothel madam.

Trust and respect on one hand, and the temptation of work in a well-paid job in Mumbai on the other, entrapped Meera in the sex trade industry. Meera spent four years in the brothel. She was rescued by Nepali NGO workers, Indian social workers, and the Indian police. She was brought back to Nepal by Nepali NGO workers. Meera's case indicates how factory work culture and living arrangements may perpetuate trafficking and the sex trade. We need to understand that with a mobile workforce and the pattern of employment of factory work – easy in and easy out and the constant flow of workers' acquaintances visiting them – young women are extremely vulnerable to trafficking and the sex industry.

Gender dynamics are unique and central to all arenas of sex trafficking and the sex trade industry. In this particular narrative, the victim/survivor, traffickers, and brothel madam were all women. Many women operate in the sex trade industry, from sex trafficking to running a brothel. There was a violation of trust between and among women. Gender was used to gain Meera's trust. Like Reeta and Tara, her local traffickers were able to easily convince her with the fake story. The narrative also indicates the magnitude of transnational practices through the partnership of local and international actors in the manifestation of such organized and illicit trade.

Conclusion

I began this paper by discussing some trends, patterns, and directions of sex trafficking in global and South Asian perspectives. Using intersectional and transnational frameworks, I analyzed the magnitude of sex trafficking of Nepali girls and women in relation to Nepal's political economy; the Indo-Nepal relationship and its geopolitics; globalization and transnational networks; women's roles and positions in Nepali society; gender ideologies; women's socioeconomic and demographic backgrounds; and women's social networks as well as their kin and ethnic relations.

These narratives illustrate the social, cultural, economic, political, historical, and global contexts of sex trafficking and the sex trade. Poverty, which has been overtly reported in previous studies, is just one contributing factor. The sex trafficking and sex trade industry is structured with multiple factors and multilevel inequalities. These factors include globalization; internal and international migration; transnational practices; family structure; patriarchal household relations; women's roles and positions in private and public domains; a gender culture of oppression; and the attraction of modern city life. The dynamics of gender, ethnicity, and social and transnational networks mediate, facilitate, and accelerate the sex trafficking process.

A gendered culture of oppression, gendered discrimination, and gender inequality were prominent and a common theme in each of the narratives. The perceptions about women as a commodity as well as their secondary position in both family and society make certain groups of women vulnerable for labor and sexual exploitation. These women are already marginalized in various other domains (e.g. socioeconomic). The majority of women in Nepal, particularly the rural poor and uneducated, still face social, economic, and political dependency on males. The religious beliefs, cultural factors, legal system, laws, and regulations for women in Nepal further exacerbate the discrimination and suppression of women. The nation's daily newspaper, *The Rising Nepal* (2003), made the following report:

> Laws and regulations in Nepal contain 156 provisions that discriminate against women. The discriminations occur in the areas of property, employment, court procedure, marriage and family, sexual harassment, citizenship forms, etc.
> Girls and women are still seen as property and a transferrable commodity that can be controlled by the patriarch of the household. Such a mindset has allowed men to sell girls and women.

However, men are not the only sex traffickers. Women are also co-opted in the process. As revealed in Meera's case, women are themselves facilitating sex trafficking. While there are unequal power relations among and between women, a gender lens alone (although important) is not adequate to analyze the experiences of the victims and survivors of sex trafficking. Intersectional and transnational frameworks have become crucial for analyzing the complexity of sex trafficking. In *Sex and Gender through the Prism of Difference*, Zinn *et al.* (2005: 3) suggested that people's lives are affected by their 'location in a number of different hierarchies'. This is also apparent in the lives of Nepali girls and women. Women's ages, class positions, gender, familial roles, relations, level of education, cultural values and beliefs, as well as regional and national locations all factor into their situation.

The narratives presented in this paper deal specifically with cross-border trading between two adjacent countries, which may make the trafficking of Nepali girls and women seem more like a South Asian regional phenomenon than a global one. The historical, geopolitical, and sociocultural relationships between Nepal and India provide favorable conditions to manifest sex trafficking between the two countries: a fluid border, no visa requirement, similar culture, language, and physical attributes, etc.

However, sex trafficking is also a manifestation of transnational networks, connections, and partnerships. The magnitude of the sex trafficking between Nepal and India indicates that more and more Nepalis and Indians operate and partner in this well-established, organized, and highly profitable industry. More recently, the newer patterns and trends of sex trafficking of Nepali girls and women illustrate that the issue is becoming increasingly global and transnational. It now encompasses different routes, nations, and actors. The Gulf nations, Southeast Asia (particularly Hong Kong), and Chinese-occupied Tibetan cities (Khasa, Kuti, and Lhasa) have become popular destinations for trafficked girls and women (personal communication with Anuradha Koirala, 2012). The social, economic, and political processes of globalization have accelerated the sex trafficking of Nepali girls and women, in which actors from various nations partner and operate together.

The women's narratives in this paper may not be so different from those reported by INGOs, NGOs, and the media. But an analysis through gender, intersectional, and transnational frameworks illustrates that trafficking and the sex trade is rooted in the multiple inequalities and the intersections of these inequalities – regional inequality, socioeconomic inequality, gender inequality, and exploitation – and the fact that it is also tied into a complex social and transnational network of people. The intersecting multilayered variables that factor into sex trafficking and the sex trade should preclude any generalizations about the conditions under which girls and women become sex workers.

Nepal is a complex, multi-stratified society where regional and socioeconomic demographics, sociocultural factors, and political and economic historical processes play a major role in determining women's roles, positions, and lived realities. Given the unique stratified structure of Nepalese society, our questions should be 'which woman?' 'how?', and 'under what social-, cultural-, economic-, familial-, community-, national-, and global-level conditions?' she is trafficked and is forced to become a sex worker.

Acknowledgements

I would like to thank the anonymous reviewers for their comments and feedback on the earlier draft of this paper. I would also like to thank all the non-governmental organizations and their staff (in particular ABC/Nepal, Maiti Nepal, and Santhi Purnasthapana Kendra) and the children's and women's cell of Kathmandu Valley Police Station in Hanuman Dhoka, Kathmandu for allowing me to conduct this study and for their help during the process. I am also thankful to Ms. Durga Ghimire, Anuradha Koirala, and Bishwo Khadka for sharing their valuable perspectives with me concerning sex trafficking and gender issues in Nepal. I would like to dedicate this article to those girls and women who shared with me their experiences with great courage and hope. Each time I conversed with them, they reopened old wounds. This study would not have been possible without their strength and vision.

Notes

[1]   Exploring these challenges is beyond the scope of this paper.
[2]   I use the terms 'victims' and 'survivors' to refer to those girls and women who were trafficked and coerced to work as prostitutes in Indian Brothels. They were victims because

they were forced to sell their sexual labor; they were also survivors as they were trying to rebuild their lives in the safe homes provided by the NGOs.

[3]   Amount of time spent in the Indian brothels was one of the main criteria for selection for narrative collections. Those who were spent at least 2–3 years in the brothels were selected.

[4]   The majority of the actual victims/survivors of sex trafficking and sex trade were being rehabilitated in the safe homes in ABC Nepal and Maiti Nepal. This was the main reason why I chose women from these NGOs for narrative collections.

[5]   Since 1959, Tibet has been occupied by China.

[6]   Actual victims/survivors refer to those who were trafficked and sold into the Indian brothels. Potential victim refers to those who were intercepted and rescued by the NGO workers and police during sex trafficking process.

[7]   In recent years, young girls are also being trafficked from the dance and cabin restaurants in Kathmandu; some of them are trafficked from circuses as well.

[8]   These husbands, however, turned out to be sex traffickers who were fishing for young and naïve girls. They used love and marriage as means to trap the girls in the sex trade.

Works Cited

Adhikari, R., 2007. Combating girl-trafficking and sex slavery. *Nepal monitor: the national online journal on media and public affairs*. Available from: http://www.nepalmonitor.com/2007/06/combating_girltraffi.html [Accessed 20 December 2013].

Bales, K., 2004. *Disposable people: new slavery in the global economy*. Los Angeles: University of California Press.

Bales, K., Trodd, Z., and Williamson, A.K., 2009. *Modern slavery: secret world of 27 million people*. Oxford: Oneworld.

Choo, H.Y. and Ferree, M.M., 2010. Practicing intersectionality in sociological research: a critical analysis of inclusions, interactions, and institutions in the study of inequalities. *Sociological theory*, 28 (2), 129–149.

Collins, P.H. 1990. *Black feminist thought: knowledge, consciousness and the politics of empowerment (perspectives on gender)*. London: Routledge.

Crawford, M., 2010. *Sex trafficking in South Asia: telling Maya's story*. London: Routledge.

Crenshaw, K. 1989. Demarginalizing the intersection of race and sex: a black feminist critique of antidiscrimination doctrine, feminist theory and antiracist politics. *University of Chicago legal forum*, 140, 139–167.

Datta, P., 2005. Nepali female migration and trafficking. *Journal of social science*, 11, 49–56.

Deane, T., 2010. Cross-border trafficking in Nepal and India-violating women's rights. *Human rights review*, 11 (4), 491–513.

Enloe, C., 1990. *Bananas, beaches, and bases: making feminist sense of international politics*. Berkeley: University of California Press.

Farr, K., 2005. *Sex trafficking: the global market in women and children*. New York: Worth.

Ghimire, D., 1994. Girl trafficking in Nepal - a situation analysis. *In*: ABC/Nepal, ed. *Red light traffic: the trade in Nepali girls*. 2nd ed. Kathmandu: ABC/Nepal, 66.

Ghimire, D., 1997. *Sexual exploitation of Nepalese girls (paper presented in the regional seminar)*. Kathmandu: ABC Nepal.

51 girls rescued from flesh trade in Khasa. 2013. *My Republica*, 28 April, kathmandu, Nepal.

Hamal Gurung, S. 2003. *Women and home-based and factory-based carpet production in Nepal: beyond formal and informal economy*. Thesis (PhD). Northeastern University.

Hamal Gurung, S. 2008. Human trafficking. *In*: J.H. Moore, ed. *Encyclopedia of race and racism*. Vol. 2. New York: Macmillan Social Science Library, 137.

Huda, S., 2006. Sex trafficking in South Asia. *International journal of gynecology & obstetrics*, 94 (3), 374–381.

Hynes, H.P. and Raymond, J.G., 2002. Put in harm's way: the neglected health consequences of sex trafficking in the United States. *In*: J. Silliman and A. Bhattacharejee, eds. *Policing the national body: race, gender, and criminalization*. Boston, MA: South End Press, 197–229.

ILO/IPEC. 2002. *Internal trafficking among children and youth engaged in prostitution.* Kathmandu: International Labor Migration/Internal Programme on the Elimination of Child Labor.

Kara, S., 2010. *Sex trafficking: inside the business of modern day slavery.* New York: Columbia University Press.

Kaufman, M. and Crawford M., 2011. Research and activism review: sex trafficking in Nepal: a review of intervention and prevention programs. *Violence against women*, 7 (5), 651–665.

Kempadoo, K., 2004. *Sexing the Caribbean.* New York: Routledge.

Limoncelli, S.A., 2008. Human Trafficking: globalization, exploitation, transnational sociology. *Sociology compass*, 2 (1), 2–20.

Limoncelli, S.A., 2009. The trouble with trafficking:conceptualizing women's sexual labor and economic human rights. *Women's studies international forum*, 32, 261–269.

McCall, L., 2001. *Complex inequality: gender, class and race in the new economy.* London and New York: Routledge.

Miller, J., 2006. Slave Trade: combating human trafficking. *Harvard international review*, 27 (4), 70–73.

Pradhan, G., 1994. The road to Bombay: forgotten women. *In*: ABC/Nepal, ed. 1996. *Red light traffic: the trade in Nepali girls*. Kathmandu: ABC/Nepal, 66.

Shelley, L. 2010. *Human trafficking: a global perspectives.* New York: Cambridge University Press.

Simkhada, P., 2008. Life histories and survival strategies amongst sexually trafficked girls in Nepal. *Children & society*, 22, 235–248.

The Rising Nepal, 2003. Laws being amended to increase women's involvement, [Editorial] 14 March, Kathmandu, Nepal.

UN.Gift.Org. (UN Global Initiative to Fight Human Trafficking), 2007. *Human trafficking: an overview*. New York, United Nations Office on Drugs and Crime. Available from: http://www.ungift.org/docs/ungift/pdf/knowledge/ebook.pdf [Accessed 20 December 2013].

United Nations Development Program (UNDP), 2009. Regional HIV, Health and Development Programme for Asia and the Pacific:HIV/AIDS and Mobility in South Asia. Available from: http://www.snap-undp.org/elibrary/Publications/HIVandMobilityInSouthAsia.pdf [Accessed 14 February 2014].

US Department of State, 2011. *Office to monitor and combat trafficking in persons. Trafficking in persons report 2011*. Available from: http://www.state.gov/j/tip/rls/tiprpt/2011/164233.htm [Accessed 20 December 2013].

Wilson, T.D., 1997. Rape for profit: trafficking of Nepali girls and women to India's brothels. *The international migration review*, 31 (2), 490–491.

Zinn, M.B., *et al.*, 2005. Introduction. *In*: M.B. Zinn, P. Hondagneu-Sotelo and M. Messner, eds. *Gender through the prism of difference*. New York: Oxford University Press, 1–10.

Sexual Exploitation and Trafficking of Women and Girls in Mexico: An Analysis on Impact of Violence on Health Status

Arun Kumar Acharya

Trafficking has a deep impact on the health and well-being of women and girls. The forms of violence, abuse, and risk that trafficked women and girls experience force them into a marginalized condition in terms of physical, mental, and sexual health. Thus, the main objective of this paper is to explore the kinds of violence faced by trafficked women and girls in Mexico City and in particular how they affect the physical and sexual health of these women. Sixty trafficked women and girls currently working as sex workers were interviewed using a semi-structured questionnaire and 28 in-depth interviews (20 trafficked women and girls, 5 madams, and 3 traffickers) conducted in Mexico City. I found that trafficked women are overwhelmingly young; little educated; unmarried; work in bars, massage parlors, and brothels; and live with a pimp. Interviewed trafficked women and girls suffer a wide range of physical and sexual violence, such as beaten with objects, sexual and verbal abuse, and cigarette burns, and are threatened with murder. Unwanted pregnancies and forced abortion are also frequent occurrences. Almost all women and girls are infected by sexually transmitted diseases.

Human trafficking is a crime that ruthlessly exploits women, children, and men for numerous purposes including forced labor and sex. This global crime generates billions of dollars in profits for the traffickers. The International Labour Organization

(ILO) estimates that around 20.9 million people are victims of forced labor globally. This estimate also includes victims of human trafficking for labor and sexual exploitation; however, it is not known that how many of these victims were trafficked (UNODC 2012). On the contrary, the 2013 Trafficking in Persons Report provided by the US Department of State indicates that as many as 27 million men, women, and children are victims of trafficking at any given time (US Department of State 2013). Global report on Trafficking in Personas-2012 indicates that globally women and girls share around 75 per cent among victims of trafficked persons, among which 58 per cent are used for sexual exploitation and 36 per cent exploited for forced labor (UNODC 2012).

In the year 2000, the United Nations in its Protocol to Prevent, Suppress, and Punish Trafficking in Persons adopted in Palermo defines human trafficking in Article 3 as:

> the recruitment, transportation, transfer, harbouring or receipt of persons, by means of threat or use of force or other forms of coercion, of abduction, of fraud, of deception, of the abuse of power or of a position of vulnerability or of the having control over another person, for the purpose of exploitation. (United Nations 2004)

This protocol cites a list of acts, which includes recruitment, transportation, and others, followed by the methods used to enforce those acts, for example threat, the use of force, or other abuses of power or of a position of vulnerability. The definition then relates to the motive: the purpose of exploitation. The definition continues by giving content to the term 'exploitation': 'Exploitation shall include, at a minimum, the exploitation of the prostitution of others or other forms of sexual exploitation, forced labor or services, slavery or practices similar to slavery, servitude or the removal of organs' (Skilbrei and Tveit 2008).

Research on trafficking of women states that young girls and women, mainly trafficked for the purpose of sexual exploitation and forced prostitution, often suffer extreme physical, sexual, and psychological exploitation, and it leads to a high risk of unwanted pregnancy and sexually transmitted infections (STIs) (Prince et al. 2007; Zimmerman et al. 2008). Raphael and Shapiro (2004), for example, indicated that trafficked women suffer an extremely elevated physical and sexual violence. Their research in Chicago on trafficked women working as escorts, exotic dancers, and prostitutes on the street and in hotels reported that women suffered different kinds of violence, such as being threatened with a weapon, physically assaulted, stabbed, kidnapped, beaten with objects, and robbed.

Goldenberg et al. (2012) studied 624 female sex workers in Tijuana and Ciudad Juarez, Mexico and found that 42 per cent were forced to enter sex work as minors and they experienced a higher prevalence of sexual violence and substance use risk, which associated with health impacts. Research of Strathdee et al. (2008) and Ojeda et al. (2009) on female sex workers at US-Mexico border indicates that majority of them are migrants and they experience high prevalence of violence, HIV, and STIs. In another study, Barton (2006) specify that experience of high levels of physical and sexual violence, harassment, and emotional strain of daily sexual activities are among the factors contributing to physical, sexual, and mental health problems among the women in sex industry, as well as that they are at risk for host of STIs beyond HIV/AIDS.

Xiang-Sheng Chen *et al.* (2005) studied 505 female sex workers in Yunnan, China and found that 84 per cent had at least one STI, 48.3 per cent had two concurrent infections, and 15 per cent had three concurrent STIs. The most prevalent STIs were caused by Chlamydia trachomatis (59 per cent), Trichomonas vaginalis (43 per cent), and Neisseria gonorrhoeae (73.2 per cent). Similarly, Farley *et al.* (2004) studied 854 trafficked women in nine countries (Canada, US, Mexico, Colombia, South Africa, Thailand, Zambia, Turkey, and Germany) and inquired about current and lifetime history of sexual and physical violence. Results indicate that 71 per cent were physically assaulted in prostitution, 63 per cent were raped, and 89 per cent of these respondents wanted to escape prostitution, but did not have other options for survival. A total of 75 per cent had been homeless at some point in their lives; 68 per cent met criteria for post-traumatic stress disorder (PTSD). Severity of PTSD symptoms was strongly associated with the number of different types of lifetime sexual and physical violence.

Above research suggest that trafficking of women and girls for sexual exploitation has recently become an important national and international issue due to growing concern about the violence against women, human rights violations including forced and exploitative labor, and spreading of STI, HIV/AIDS. In Mexico, I have observed that during the last two decades the problem of trafficking in persons especially of women and girls has undergone some deep changes: first, Mexico has become an origin, destination, and transit country for international trafficking, and second, it has the most significant incidence of growing internal trafficking compared to other Latin American countries (Cacho 2010; Seelke 2013; US Department of State 2013).

Trafficking of women and girls in Mexico is difficult to ascertain as there is little empirical data available. To date there are no official statistics on the trafficking of women, yet Teresa Ulloa, President of Regional Coalition Against Trafficking of Women and Children in Latin America and Caribbean (CATWLAC in Spanish), has claimed that every day 400 women enter into prostitution (this figure includes trafficked and non-trafficked women) in Mexico City and of these 80 per cent enter against their will (González 2003). Trafficking of women and girls in Mexico especially for Mexico City is poorly understood as there is lack of research available. Though some civil organizations — for example *CATWLAC, Infancia Común, Colectivo contra la Trata de Personas* among others — are working hard to combat trafficking in Mexico City, the scale and consequences of the practice are not well understood.

Thus, taking the above into account, I formulated the following research questions: how does the trafficking of women and girls develop in Mexico City? What are the forms of violence faced by trafficked women and girls in their daily life? How does this violence affect physical and sexual health of trafficked women? Based on these questions, our main objective of this paper is to explore the kinds of violence faced by trafficked women and girls and in particular how they affect the physical and sexual health of these women.

Methodology

Trafficked women are treated as a hidden population, for whom it is notoriously difficult to establish a reliable sampling frame. This tends to make randomized sampling strategies unsuitable. Thus, the snowball sampling technique was used during the fieldwork for this paper. The location of trafficked women and interviews were carried out in two steps. The first step was contact with a key informant and the second step was interviews with trafficked women.

Step 1: Information from a Key Informant

In Mexico City, I contacted the Instituto de las Mujeres del DF (Institute of Women of Federal District) to get information on trafficked women. The director of the institute claimed that at that moment they did not have any information as they were conducting extensive research on domestic violence, but they put me in touch with Maria, a 40 – 45 year-old sex worker in Mexico City. I contacted Maria and told her about my project and after several meetings, she said that she would try to help, but as it is difficult for her to move from one place to another she might not be able to locate many trafficked women. After few months Maria contacted me over telephone and gave me information of a trafficked woman and the name of the brothel where she worked.

Step 2: Interview with Trafficked Women

After getting the information, we (Patricio Villalva, Ph.D candidate at the Instituto de Investigaciones Antropologicas, National Autonomous University of Mexico and myself) went to the designated brothel and contacted the woman, we told her the nature of our study and mentioned that Maria had given us her name and location. After few minutes of conversation, we paid the solicited amount (200 pesos[1] for 30 minutes) to hide our identity in front of the brothel owner and traffickers and went to a private room to talk more freely. Only the trafficked woman had knowledge that we were researchers. After termination of the interviews, we asked her to help us find other trafficked women who are working in the same or nearby brothels. In the beginning she declined to help, but after regular interaction she agreed to cooperate with us to locate other trafficked women. We also promised to pay her 100 pesos (8 USD) per woman in exchange. Whenever she located a woman, she arranged an interview and called us. In this way, applying the snowball technique we were able to gain access and interview trafficked women in Mexico City.

Before and during the interviews, we followed the World Health Organization (WHO) ethical and safety recommendations for interviewing trafficked women authored by Zimmerman and Watts (2003), including the relevant ethical and methodological procedures such as protection of participant confidentiality, anonymity, and safety. It is also necessary to mention that all interviewees were voluntary participants in this study and knew of the risks and benefits.

Moreover, at the beginning of the interview, we invited the interviewees to come to our house or to any other location, but they always responded with 'no'. They would tell us '[…] this is our area; it is not possible for us to go out from this place, because madrina (madam) do not permit us to work in other places […]'. Since women were not allowed to leave the brothel, we acted as 'clients' as it was the only way we were able to gain access. Interviews lasted for around 30 minutes and using the snowball technique we interviewed a total of 60 women with semi-structured questionnaire to know the causes and consequences of trafficking. All interviews were conducted in Spanish, audio-taped, and carried out during 2003 – 2006.

We also conducted 28 in-depth interviews, which included 20 trafficked women (15 women were less than 18 years old, 3 women were between 18 and 20 years, and another two women were 23 years and 27 years, respectively), 5 madams, and three traffickers. All interviews with madams and traffickers were organized by Maria. The main objective of these interviews was to know more about the life history of the trafficked women, madam, and traffickers. Interviews were later transcribed and the participants' names replaced with unique pseudonyms to protect their identities. For the purpose of this research we considered trafficked women and girls who were less than 18 years or older and trafficked according to the Trafficking Protocol definition.

Trafficking of Women and Sex Industry in Mexico

Hundreds of thousands of persons are trafficked across international borders annually from Latin America; it is one of the most under-researched practices among issues of sexual exploitation (Cicero-Domínguez 2005), and Mexico is a large source, transit, and destination country for trafficked persons (US Department of State 2013). Studies conducted by Peña (2013) and Carreño (2009) indicates that complex social and economic factors, including those related to migration, human rights abuses, poverty, gender inequalities, and organized crime, are believed to contribute to vulnerability, exploitation, and adolescent sex work in Mexico.

Evidence suggests that sexual exploitation and involvement in sex work causes serious health-related harms among marginalized women and girls. For example, studies by Decker *et al.* (2011), Silverman (2011), and Sarkar *et al.* (2008) specify that women who are trafficked for the purpose of sexual exploitation are greatly vulnerable to sexual and physical violence, STIs, and HIV infection. The research conducted by Sarkar *et al.* (2008) on sex trafficking and HIV infection among sex workers in eastern India found that around 25 per cent of sex workers reported that they had been forced or deceived to exchange sex; these participants were more likely to report violence when they began to exchange sex, which was associated with higher risk of HIV infection.

Torres Mendoza *et al.* (1988) studied the health issues of 670 commercial sex workers in Guadalajara city, Mexico and found that only 3 (0.44 per cent) were seropositive. All three women were working in a nightclub that served clients with high socioeconomic status. These women all had generalized lymphadenopathy and two had a history of blood transfusions. On the whole, the findings indicate that 70 per cent of women had vaginal intercourse, 34 per cent engaged in oral sex, and 9 per cent reported regular anal intercourse. The three sex workers who were seropositive did not use condoms during the vaginal intercourse whereas they rarely engaged with anal and oral sex. Valdespino *et al.* (1990) interviewed 3612 commercial sex workers in 20 Mexican cities and results indicated that 0.4 per cent of women were HIV positive. In the year 1999, National Council for Prevention and Control of AIDS (CONASIDA – Consejo Nacional para Prevención y Control del SIDA) conducted an HIV test among 1915 commercial sex workers in Mexico City and found that the HIV positive prevalence rate is 0.36 per cent (CONASIDA 1999).

Similarly, Conde Gonzalez studied the prevalence of sexually transmitted diseases among commercial sex workers in Mexico City. Their study found that 10.1 per cent of women had syphilis, 9 per cent had been infected by anti-HBc, 69.8 per cent by simple herpes type-2, 2.1 per cent by gonorrhea, and 23.7 per cent by chlamydia (Conde Gonzalez *et al.* 1993). In 1993, Juarez and others of INSP (Instituo Nacional de Salud Pública) interviewed 495 commercial sex workers and found that 48.9 per cent had the human papillomavirus (HPV) and 43 per cent had cancer cervicouter-ino (Secretaria de Salud 1993). All the studies demonstrate that women working as commercial sex workers are very much exposed to the infection of RTI, STI, and HIV. Hence the problem needs a better understanding about its dynamics and scope and extent of the health risks. As in other parts of the world, the trafficking of women for the purpose of prostitution is becoming an increasingly lucrative business in Mexico where women from the poorest regions are particularly at risk of being abused (Acharya and Stevanato 2005).

It should come as no surprise that women are particularly vulnerable to the nexus between trafficking and STI like HIV. The approach of national public health institutions to STI and HIV increasingly recognizes that women's vulnerability to HIV is integrally connected with discrimination and violence. Today, this has become an important subject for politicians, academicians, and for the general public due to its consequences on public health and the rapid changes in the number of HIV patients. For example, in the year 2001, in general, in Mexico there were 50,776 persons living with HIV, which increased to 64,483 after just one year in 2002. Whereas in 2003 it was 71,584 cases, in 2004 it was 93,855 and in 2005 it reached 102,575 cases, where 20 per cent of all these identified cases were from Mexico City (Secretaria de Salud 2005). These data provide a glimpse of the serious epidemic of STI, like HIV that the country is experiencing. Some of the important factors contributing to this increasing number are unprotected heterosexual behavior and the growing sex market in various Mexican cities including Mexico City.

Other studies on trafficking, for instance by Silverman (2011), Silverman *et al.* (2006), Kempadoo and Doezema (1998), Global Alliance Against Traffic in Women (GAATW) (2001), and Binh (2006) have identified that this business is associated with a high health risk primarily due to lack of access to services, isolation, and exploitative working conditions. The trafficking of women for sexual exploitation is accompanied by potentially lifelong and/or life-threatening health consequences. It prevents victims from attaining the highest possible level of physical, mental, and social wellbeing. It is necessary to address the health implications of trafficking, because this process itself becomes a health hazard, where victims' health is further endangered in situations of sexual exploitation.

General Characteristics of Trafficked Women and Girls

It is very difficult to underline a specific cause for trafficking in Mexico, but this study concludes that the trafficking of women and girls is a result of 'multicausal factors'. During the interviews women cited a wide range of factors such as unemployment, poverty, domestic violence, desertion by a spouse, and ethnic conflict that pushed them toward trafficking. Traffickers tailor their promises to these problems experienced by women. From the responses it is clear that women are largely lured through false promises, such as employment with good remuneration as well as an exotic life in the US, and once traffickers trap them with these promises, they never take them to the US and only move them to Mexico City to work in prostitution. Most of them became aware of the real work at the intermediary place or destination.

Once a trafficker takes a woman out of her place of origin, he puts her in different intermediaries places and uses different kinds of training, which includes how she has to work; the way to negotiate with clients; kinds of dress she will wear; how she has to perform the sexual relation(s); and other rules and regulations of brothel like not to leave the brothel without the permission of owner and not to talk and give any self/personal information, as well as that of others, to anybody. After learning the real purpose of their migration, if they do not accept the new job that the pimps and traffickers have obligated them to, various kind of violence would be used to coerce the women. This aggression does not end at the intermediary place, it continues until a trafficked woman reaches the brothel. Many women stated that after leaving their house, their life was converted into a life of violence. This kind of violence has lots of impacts on the health of women.

The research here indicates that trafficked women were significantly younger; the majority of them are below the age of 25 years. I hardly found any women over 25 years of age. On the other hand, nearly 70 to 75 per cent of women were younger than 18 years of age (see Table 1). This is an important characteristic of this illicit market, where only young women are taken into consideration. Effectively, pimps do not prefer women who are older. According to one brothel owner, '[…] woman after the 25 years old is considered old and aged for this industry and also clients do not prefer this kind of woman […].'

In terms of their marital status, I found that the majority of trafficked women were unmarried. There were fewer numbers of married women who were currently separated from their husband. This reflects that majority of the trafficked women were single or 'unmarried' women, as a pimp said: '[…] I do not want to buy a

Table 1 Demographic characteristics of trafficked women and girls in Mexico.

Demographic characteristics	Per cent	Number
Current age		
Less than 18 years	72.2	57
18–25 years	18.8	15
More than 25 years	10.0	8
Marital status		
Unmarried	78.7	63
Single mother/divorced	15.0	12
Married	6.3	5
Ethnic group		
Indigenous	28.7	23
Mestizo	71.3	57

married woman even a divorced woman, because for me she is just like a used cloth, where she does not have the same smell like a new one […].'

It is important to point out that the brothel is treated as a market, where victims are considered as commodities, and each aspect depends on loss and gain based on supply and demand. For example, if a pimp buys a 20-year-old married or divorced woman, she is less preferred by clients, which is not as profitable for the pimp. A 20 year old will only provide approximately 4 – 5 years of service (as women older than 25 years are considered too old in this business). Whereas, if a pimp buys a 15–year-old woman or younger, she can easily provide services for the pimp for a minimum of 7 to 8 years. Also, the demand is higher as young women, generating a higher profit for the pimp. So, in total a brothel owner will gain more money from a young unmarried woman than an older married woman.

Looking into the other demographic characteristics of the trafficked women, the majority of interviewed trafficked women were mestizo ethnic group (Spanish mixed race) and the rest were indigenous (see Table 1). The question is *why were more women mestizo?* After the conversation with some pimps and traffickers I learnt that mestizo women are highly preferred by the clients because of their white skin color. One pimp said '[…] clients do not want to have the sex with a dark skin girl, they do not prefer indigenous women, though I can buy an indigenous woman at a cheaper price than a mestizo, but on her my (economic) gain is very marginal […].'

Aggression and Violence Faced by Trafficked Women and Girls

As we have seen from our earlier discussion, women and girls are forced into prostitution and it is very common to see that these women face a wide range of aggressions and violence from the pimp, traffickers, and to some extent from clients. Research indicates that trafficked women experience high levels of violence, such as physical assaults, sexual assaults, verbal threats or abuse, and psychological abuse (Lowman 2000; Raymond 2004). According to Zimmerman *et al.* (2009), trafficked women live in a very hazardous environment; it is not because of lower hygienic condition, but due to the clandestine condition, exploitation, violence they face, and lack of access to health care.

During the interviews and analyses, I clearly observed that the incidence of both physical and sexual violence at the hand of traffickers and pimps is a common event in the life of these trafficked women. The women and girls were exposed to a wide range of violence during the one week that past between interviews. The violence consisted of: being beaten with an object, abused verbally, and locked in a room without food. Some women and girls also said that they were burned with cigarettes, threaten to be killed by the madam, and a number of women reported that the madam put chili powder in their eyes and vagina, as well as forced them to have sex with more than one client at a time. This clearly indicates the incidence of violence against women and the level of extreme cruel and inhumane treatment.

For example, one woman said:

> [...] for us violence is common, it is nothing new, we are habituated on this, here we do not have right of our body, here we treated just like an animal, it is madrina (madam) who decide all for us, when we have to work, with whom we have to work, what to do or not, when we have to eat, sleep etc., all these depend on her, we do not have right to tell a 'no', if we do not follow her words she just use her power in many ways, for her our life is nothing, in this place her dog has more respect than us [...].

Thus, once the women are coerced into this profession their life is in danger. In sum, this exploitation makes them victims and exposes them to ill health.

Sexual Behavior of Trafficked Women and Girls

Sexual behavior of trafficked woman and girls is very important as it is closely related with their sexual health. It also encompasses the problems of HIV and STIs/RTIs, unintended pregnancy and abortion, infertility and cancer resulting from STIs, and sexual dysfunction. The sexual behavior of women in commercial sex can be accessed through the number of clients they receive in a day and according to their typical sexual relation. To get a complete idea of the sexual behavior of trafficked women various questions were asked during the interviews.

From the information collected it is clear that the majority of women receive more than 10 clients a day, although there were some women who received less than five clients a day. So, to find out more on this differential characteristic, I did a bi-variate analysis, which indicated an inverse relationship between the age of the women and number of clients. As the age of the women and girls increases the number of clients per day decreases, according to the clients preferences outlined earlier. Similarly, the clients avoided the women who had been working in the brothel for many years as clients assumed these women would be more likely to have been infected by various sexually transmitted diseases.

Apart from the above, in order to get a full picture of the sexual behavior of the trafficked women, I asked whether their clients used condoms during their sexual relation, and if so, how frequently. We also asked how many types of physical relations they practiced with their clients. On the basis of these questions, I can report that for the majority of women and girls their clients do not use a condom at the time of sex. This information shows how vulnerable this population is to infection via sexual intercourse. When examining the reason for this, I found that it is not that the women or girls who do not want to have safe sex, but it is the pimp who forces them to have sex without condom with the intention of earning more money. When a girl has sex without condom, the client pays more money. So, in these cases it is impossible for women and girls to negotiate with the client for a safe sex. On the other hand, I have seen from the responses that trafficked women were forced to exercise a wide range of sexual activity at a time as per the demand of clients. Majority of the practices at a time were vaginal, oral, and anal sex.

Health Disorder and Reproductive Health Status

The severity of violence and the environment where these women and girls are living can also be assessed for incidences of unwanted pregnancy and forced abortion. From the data collected nearly half the number of women were exposed to unwanted pregnancy and had been given an abortion. During the conversation with trafficked women and girls, I found that in very few cases the abortion was carried out in a clinic. Abortions carried out in a clinic only took place when the madam came to know about the pregnancy in its late stage. While in the other cases, women reported that when their madam came to know about their pregnancy after two or three weeks she gave some medicines and few days after they lost their pregnancy.

The precarious living environment, nutrient deficiency, insufficient physical rest, and intense physical and psychological violence result in a high incidence of illness and suffering among the trafficked women and girls. The most common health problem among the trafficked women being fever, backache, sleep disorder, irregular menstruation, stomach and back pain during menstruation, heavy bleeding during menstruation, pain during intercourse, bleeding after intercourse, lower abdominal pain, abnormal vaginal discharge, and burning sensation while passing urine.

As reported earlier, only in very rare cases was safe sex an option for the trafficked women and girls, moreover they were exposed to very subhuman working conditions. They did not have access to good medical facilities; if they experience health problems the madam is the only person who will take them to a clinic (which is usually located near the brothel). As far as the information obtained during the field work is concerned, most of these clinics were fake. There are numerous drug stores located near brothels, where they sell imitation of many medicines as well as medicine with expired dates at a cheaper price. If a woman reported her health problem to the madam, first, the madam would give some kind of medicine and in the case of emergency she would be taken to clinic. But, before going to clinic, the madam would threaten them to ensure that they do not give any information about their workplace to the clinician. After returning from the clinic, the madam would never show the clinic bill, but would just mention to the woman that she spent a lot of money and ask her to repay the sum by taking more clients. The women accept what madam says as they do not have other options.

Discussion

The above discussion gives a clear picture that no one in Mexico could be more vulnerable to sexual violence than the women and girls pushed into trafficking. It has been suggested throughout this study, the health consequences are commonly severe and long lasting among trafficked women. The trauma of sexual coercion and assault at different stages of their life cycle leaves many of these women with severe loss of self-esteem and autonomy. This, in turn, means that they do not always make the best sexual and reproductive health decisions for themselves. Many of them accept victimization as 'part of being female.'

The trafficked women and girls in Mexico City are extremely vulnerable in every aspect. Not only do they run serious risks of physical and sexual violence, but they have also been stigmatized as carrying the main responsibility for the spreading of sexually transmitted diseases and HIV/AIDS. Basically, these women and girls' ability to protect themselves from STDs and HIV/AIDS is drastically weakened by the threat of madam's violence; also their ability to negotiate condom use by their male partners is inversely related to the extent or degree of abuse in their relationship.

While the results of this study cannot be representative of Mexico because of its limited sample size, this study has documented and sheds some light on the level of sexual and physical violence against the trafficked women and it underlines the need to address safety for sex workers, which are caught up with issues of legality and social stigma. Likewise, the economic and social conditions that create the necessity for trafficking have been neglected, but are vital to address if women are to have other viable options to support themselves and their family.

These days, trafficking of women and girls cuts across social and economic conditions deeply embedded in the cultures around the world, where millions of women and girls consider it a way of life. This kind of violence against women rarely results in finite consequences that can be addressed with a prescriptive or band-aid approach. Trafficking harms women and girls in insidious ways that create 'messy' health problems. The physical and mental health consequences are not a side effect of trafficking, but a central theme.

This study suggests that the trafficking of women and girls is now an issue of global dimensions, which requires an urgent and concerted response. The gravity of the situation has sent shock waves in Mexican society due to the AIDS pandemic. A comprehensive approach is essential to address the economic, social, and political aspects of women trafficking. It is necessary to deal with the perpetrators, as well as to assist the victim of trafficking.

Acknowledgments

This research was funded by Ministry of Foreign Affairs-Mexico through doctoral fellowship during 2002–2006.

Note

[1]   16 USD.

Works Cited

Acharya, A.K. and Stevanato, A.S., 2005. Violencia y tráfico de mujeres en México: Una perspectiva de Género [Violence and trafficking of women in Mexico: a gender perspectives]. *Estudos Feministas*, 13 (3), 507–524.

Barton, B., 2006. *Stripped: inside the lives of exotic dancers*. New York: New York University Press.

Binh, V.N., 2006. Trafficking of women and children in Vietnam: current issues and problems. *In*: K. Beeks and D. Amir, eds. *Trafficking and the global sex industry*. Lanham, MD: Lexington Books, 33–43.

Cacho, L., 2010. *Esclavas del poder: Un viaje al corazón de la trata sexual de mujeres y niñas en el mundo* [Slaves of power: a journey to the heart of world sex trafficking of women and girls]. Mexico: Random House Mondadori.

Carreño, S.S., 2009. Legislación nacional contra la trata de personas [National laws against trafficking of persons]. *In*: C.R. Rodolfo, ed. *Rostros Diversos de la Trata de Personas en México: Situaciones Presentes y Potenciales de las Mujeres, Niñas, Niños y Adolescentes* [Different faces of human trafficking in Mexico: present and potential situation of women, children and adolescents]. México: LX Legislatura, H. Cámara de Diputados, 156–185.

Centro Naciónal Para la Prevención y el Control del VIH y el SIDA (CONASIDA) [National Center for the Prevention and Control of HIV and AIDS], 1999. *Reportes de Actividades de Conasida, 1994–1999* [Activities Reports of Conasida 1994–1999], Mexico: Department of Health, Government of Mexico.

Cicero-Domínguez, A., 2005. Assessing the U.S.-Mexico fight against human trafficking and smuggling: unintended results of U.S. immigration policy. *Northwestern journal of international human rights*, 4 (2), 303.

Conde Gonzalez, C. *et al.*, 1993. STD's prevalence studies among different populations in Mexico City. *Ninth international conference on AIDS*, June, Vol. II, abstract PO-C20-3070:729, Berlin, Germany: International AIDS Society, 729.

Decker, M.R. *et al.*, 2011. Sex trafficking, sexual risk, sexually transmitted infection and reproductive health among female sex workers in Thailand. *Journal of epidemiology and community health*, 65 (4), 334–339.

Farley, M. *et al.*, 2004. Prostitution and trafficking in nine countries: an update on violence and posttraumatic stress disorder. *Journal of trauma practice*, 2 (3–4), 33–74.

Global Alliance against Traffic in Women (GAATW), 2001. *Human rights and trafficking in persons: a handbook*. Bangkok: GAATW.

Goldenberg, S.M. *et al.*, 2012. Exploring the impact of underage sex work among female sex workers in two Mexico–US border cities. *AIDS and behavior*, 16 (4), 969–981.

González, R., 2003. *Violencia contra las mujeres deja un millón de víctimas anuales en México* [Annually violence against women has one million victims in Mexico]. Mexico: CIMAC.

Kempadoo, K. and Doezema, J. eds., 1998. *Global sex workers: rights, resistance, and redefinition*. New York: Routledge.

Lowman, J., 2000. Violence and the outlaw status of (street) prostitution in Canada. *Violence against women*, 6 (9), 987–1011.

Ojeda, V.D. *et al.*, 2009. Associations between migrant status and sexually transmitted infections among female sex workers in Tijuana, Mexico. *Sexually transmitted infections*, 85 (6), 420–426.

Peña, C.P.J., 2013. *La Trata de Personas en México desde la Perspectiva de las Organizaciones de la Sociedad Civil, la Academia y el Estado* [Trafficking in persons in Mexico from the perspective of civil society organizations, academy and the state]. Mexico: Puebla.

Prince, M. *et al.*, 2007. No health without mental health. *The lancet*, 370 (9590), 859–877.

Raphael, J. and Shapiro, D.L., 2004. Violence in indoor and outdoor prostitution venues. *Violence against women*, 10 (2), 126–139.

Raymond, J.G., 2004. Prostitution on demand: legalizing the buyers as sexual consumers. *Violence against women*, 10 (10), 1156–1186.

Sarkar, K. *et al.*, 2008. Sex-trafficking, violence, negotiating skill, and HIV infection in brothel-based sex workers of eastern India, adjoining Nepal, Bhutan, and Bangladesh. *Journal of health population nutrition*, 26 (2), 223.

Secretaria de Salud, 1993 [Department of Health, 1993]. *Informe de labores 1992–1993. Capítulo 3.31.7*. Mexico: Programa de Prevención y Control del Síndrome de Inmunodeficiencia Adquirida (SIDA).

Secretaria de Salud, 2005 [Department of Health, 2005]. *Programa Epidemiológico del VIH/SIDA e ITS en México*. Mexico: Centro Nacional para la prevención y control del VIH/SIDA (CONASIDA).

Seelke, C.R., 2013. *Trafficking in persons in Latin America and the Caribbean*. Washington, DC: Congressional Research Service. CRS Report for Congress, Prepared for Members and Committees of Congress, 7-5700, RL33200.

Silverman, J.G. *et al.*, 2006. HIV prevalence and predictors among rescued sex-trafficked women and girls in Mumbai, India. *JAIDS journal of acquired immune deficiency syndromes*, 43 (5), 588–593.

Silverman, J.G., 2011. Adolescent female sex workers: invisibility, violence and HIV. *Archives of disease in childhood*, 96 (5), 478–481.

Skilbrei, M.-L. and Tveit, M., 2008. Defining trafficking through empirical work: blurred boundaries and their consequences. *Gender, technology and development*, 12 (1), 9–30.

Strathdee, S.A. *et al.*, 2008. Characteristics of female sex workers with US clients in two Mexico-US border cities. *Sexually transmitted diseases*, 35 (3), 263–268.

Torres Mendoza, B. *et al.*, 1988. Prevalence of antibodies to HIV in prostitutes in Guadalajara, Mexico. *Fourth international conference on AIDS*, June, abstract 5080:332, Stockholm: International AIDS Society.

United Nations, 2004. *United Nations Convention against Transnational Organized Crime and the protocols thereto*. Vienna: United Nations Office on Drugs and Crime. Available from: http://www.unodc.org/documents/treaties/UNTOC/Publications/TOC%20Convention/TOC ebook-e.pdf [Accessed 6 Jan 2014].

United Nations Office on Drugs and Crime (UNODC), 2012. *Global report on trafficking in persons 2012*, Vienna: Research and Trend Analysis Branch Division for Policy Analysis and Public Affairs, United Nations Office on Drugs and Crime, ISBN: 978-92-1-130309-4.

US Department of State, 2013. *Trafficking in persons report-2013*. Washington, DC: US Department of State. Available from: http://www.state.gov/j/tip/rls/tiprpt/ [Accessed 6 Jan 2014].

Valdespino, J.L. *et al.*, 1990. Profile of female prostitution in Mexico and HIV Risk factor. *Sixth international conference on AIDS*, 20–24 June, abstract Th.D.51:146, San Francisco, CA: International AIDS Society.

Xiang-Sheng, C. *et al.*, 2005. Sexually transmitted infections among female sex workers in Yunnan, China. *AIDS patient care and STDs*, 19 (12), 853–860.

Zimmerman, C. *et al.*, 2008. The health of trafficked women: a survey of women entering post trafficking services in Europe. *American journal of public health*, 98 (1), 55–59.

Zimmerman, C. Kiss, L. Hossain, M. and Watts, C., 2009. *Trafficking in persons: a health concern? Ciência & Saúde Coletiva*, 14 (4), 1029–1035.

Zimmerman, C. and Watts, C., 2003. *WHO ethical and safety recommendations for interviewing trafficked women*. Geneva: World Health Organization.

The Forgotten Family: Labour Migration and the Collapse of Traditional Values in Thailand's Tribal Communities

Scott Downman

Rural communities in northern Thailand have been decimated in recent years as a direct consequence of labour migration. This migration has placed unprecedented pressure on the traditional social and cultural values within tribal communities in Thailand's north. These changes have meant the most vulnerable members of these communities – children and the elderly – are facing dilemmas and challenges unimaginable a decade ago. Among the issues to emerge as a result of labour migration are: homelessness among the elderly, changes to traditional forms of aged care, and grandparent and extended family guardianship of children. There are increasing numbers of child-headed households in villages as parents have moved in search of work. These factors have resulted in an escalation of youth-based violence and have local authorities seeking urgent solutions to address the social and cultural vacuum. This research focuses on the impacts work migration has on 'sending communities' by providing case studies from three villages in Thailand's Nan Province. The paper will argue that temporary work migration either within nations or inter-nationally, has destructive repercussions for sending communities. It will be argued that this type of migration in Thailand is instrumental in eroding ethnic pride and a loss of indigenous culture. The research was collected during fieldwork in Thailand during the past three years, two of which were spent as a full-time community development worker in an AusAID-funded project aimed at building the capacity of tribal youth leaders.

In recent years, there has been a widespread focus on the global patterns and consequences of migration. Experiences of migration can be both positive and negative depending on the circumstances surrounding the act of migration. Migration is commonly associated with the pursuit of opportunity, employment, education and hope. However, it is also associated with human trafficking, labour exploitation and organised crime. The rapidly emerging field of migration studies is undeniably complex and this research will further emphasise this complexity by providing case studies of three communities in northern Thailand. Much of the scholarship in recent years has focused on the migrants, that is, the people who migrate. The research has centred on subjects such as: the reasons for migration, the places people migrate from and the method and manner of their migration. However, little research has been done on the remnant population, the group left behind in the so-called 'sending communities' that provide migrants. Although studies of this nature have increased in the past four years, there is still a large degree of mystery about the circumstances and issues surrounding those left behind. This research 'black hole' is somewhat surprising given that this group often includes the most vulnerable members of any community – children and the elderly.

This research investigates the consequences for those that remain by providing examples from three villages that have been decimated by migration. It will be argued that modern patterns of migration within these tribal communities have created issues and problems that were unimaginable a decade ago. These include issues such as: child-headed households, youth-based violence, drug and substance abuse, suicide and aged care issues. It will be argued that cultural and social values in some of these villages have been eroded to the point where some locals are calling for vigilantism to help restore order to these communities. Research generally purports that migration is a phenomenon centred on the migration of one or both parents. This assumption, although mostly accurate, simplifies the complex interfaces associated with migration. In northern Thailand's tribal communities, migration is not just limited to care providers and adults, but rather involves whole families, often separating and leaving for different destinations and for different reasons. For example, adults may migrate for employment, financial reward or to escape poverty, while children might migrate for the purpose of receiving an education. In its most positive form it is seen as a sacrifice for the collective good of a family, but in its negative form is associated with death, family breakdown, cultural confusion and community chaos.

Significance of the Research

Investigating the 'forgotten families' of migrants in Thailand should be a crucial area of research and social intervention. However, it is not. Child rights advocates in Thailand have now labelled the children in this group as Thailand's 'invisible children' (Downman 2008). This underrepresented group in Thai society suffer silently and face a range of issues additional to those mentioned earlier including premature death, exploitation and malnutrition. Advocates have coined the term 'invisible children' because they say that the children, who are a product of migration, have no way of voicing their struggle and sharing their circumstances. This research is significant in that it attempts to give these children a voice and to share their struggles and concerns about the migration phenomenon. This research will also document the impacts of migration on the elderly. This research however, is not just about migration. It includes a study of the importance of intergenerational ties and its link with social and cultural change in a community. Lüscher and Pillemer (1998) argue that insufficient attention has been paid to social change as a factor in intergenerational ties. It has been argued that an understanding of the issues and problems older people and their families face must be examined in the context of larger processes of change (Teo *et al.* 2003: 328). This is highly pertinent in terms of holistically evaluating the impacts of migration on remnant communities.

Lyttleton (2005) in his research into tribal communities in north-west Laos refers to these issues as 'social suffering'. He argues that although migration has brought material success it has also greatly affected tribal communities. He argues some of the affects on remnant communities have included: vulnerability to HIV infection, changing forms of drug abuse and forms of psychic malaise (Lyttleton 2005: 47). These social changes have great impacts on the functions and mechanics of any community. They impact factors such as leadership, social cohesion, unity and sustainability. Yeoh *et al.* (2005) argues that further research is needed in order to gain a better understanding of the relationship between migration and health and how they are manifest across diverse socio-cultural environments. De Haan (2006) argues that although much has been written on the links between migration and poverty, the family dynamics of migration have long been overlooked. He says:

> This is surprising as the household or family seems to be key to decision-making processes around migration, and family dynamics are key to the way different individuals benefit or suffer from engagement in labour markets and employment. (de Haan 2006: 107)

This research aims to contribute to this sphere by looking at the direct impacts migration has on families remaining in the sending communities. In the past in these communities, the family unit has been pivotal in providing the basic necessities of life: shelter, food and security. In recent years however, the provision of these 'basic needs' has become the responsibility not just of the family, but also of others such as non-governmental organisations (NGOs) and charities. The consequences of this shift have been massive not only for the family unit but also for the broader community. The traditional notions of what it means to be a family have been challenged and questioned as a direct result of spiralling migration in sending communities in Thailand. Changes to intergenerational ties have altered cultural traditions and expectations, with traditional responsibilities often no longer being met. This has created a void in the lives of those living in remnant communities.

Castles (2000) points out that migration studies have suffered as a consequence of the distinction found in the literature between international migration and internal or domestic migration. This paper will focus on internal or domestic migration and will argue that despite the destination of those migrating, the consequences for remnant communities are unchanged. It must also be highlighted that the research deficiencies regarding culture in relation to migration are significantly magnified in communities with ethnic minorities. Castles (2000) links migration with globalisation and argues that this has profound consequences on culture and society. Although Castles presents a broad-scale, macro argument with regard to issues of culture, this paper adopts a more micro approach by examining the impacts of migration on the traditional, ethnic culture of specific minority communities. The paper links social change, with cultural change. Schloenhardt (2008) argues that migration is a complex phenomenon that can result from political, socio-economic, demographic, environmental, structural, historical and cultural factors. In Thailand, migration is widespread and affects regional communities across the country, but it is the ethnic minority communities, located high in the mountains and often extremely remote, which have suffered most as a consequence of migration. Lewis and Lewis argue:

> Although they [tribal communities] work hard and some receive benefits from development programmes, most tribal people face serious economic problems due to: lack of funds with which to purchase land, lack of capital with which to diversify their agriculture; and constant exposure to economic loss from robbery and exploitation. (1998: 291)

This highlights why migration has become such a high priority option for Thailand's tribal communities and also explains why remnant communities are at great risk, facing unprecedented threats to their future.

Approach and Methodology

The data collection for this research occurred during June 2007 and June 2009. The research used a holistic approach to overcome issues that can stem from a too narrow focus. Castles (2000) argues that migration studies are often conducted with a degree of fragmentation. For example, he argues that migration research is often divided into fields of study such as economics or sociology. He points out that migration research outcomes consequently vary greatly depending on the approach used by the researcher.

> The fragmentation into fields of study conflicts with the lived reality of migrants, who experience migration, settlement, ethnic relations, public policies, language issues and identity construction as closely related and overlapping segments of a single process. (Castles 2000: 15)

Depicting the lived reality of the research participants, should ultimately override a preconceived focus or agenda. However, often it does not. Because this research was conducted as part of a holistic community development project, the data collection process involved an interdisciplinary approach by which community-based economies, culture, education, sociology and environment were all considered.

During the research phase, data was collected while the principal researcher was working as a consultant on a youth-based community development project in Nan Province, northern Thailand. The data was collected using innovative, participatory data collection methods, some of which fall outside traditional forms of quantitative and qualitative methodologies and research methods. This alternative approach was deliberately adopted in tribal communities as a method of overcoming issues related to the vulnerable target groups making up the research. The target groups in this research are from three communities, in three separate districts, in two provinces. The research sample is target communities in the community development project the principal investigator was working with. Each of the target communities is vulnerable or identified as 'at-risk' to broad-scale issues including: poverty, lack of food security, unemployment and underemployment, lack of educational opportunities, drug and alcohol abuse, violence and cultural erosion.

These issues have resulted in large numbers of people migrating from these villages in search of a better life. Within these communities, most people who migrate move to urban areas within Thailand, to Bangkok or Chiang Mai. There are also some examples, however, of transnational migration to South Korea, Hong Kong and Taiwan – including examples where migrant workers are smuggled, exploited and sometimes killed as a consequence of poor working conditions in destination countries.

The main focus of this research is the impacts of domestic migration on vulnerable community members 'left behind' – children and the elderly. Within the three target communities, it is not unusual for both parents to migrate, leaving the eldest child in their family as the principal guardian of their siblings, or alternatively, placing the children into the care of grandparents or other extended family members. Because of the sensitive nature of the research subject, creative and performative methodologies were used as a mechanism to give the research participants a voice. Haseman argues:

> Over the past decade a number of qualitative researchers have drawn the same conclusion. Constrained by the capacity of words to capture the nuances and subtleties of human behaviour, some researchers have used other symbolic forms to represent their claims to knowledge. (2006: 102)

He argues that this performative methodology is characterised by non-numeric data that uses symbolic data rather than words and can include moving images of music and sound and other creative forms (Haseman 2006: 102). This approach is particularly relevant to the way data was collected at a village-based level as part of the research project. It must also be highlighted that although these approaches are relatively new in academe, they have been widely used within the community development/NGO sector with great success for many years. The advantage of these research methods is they take into account child participation, potential power imbalances between the researcher and research participants, the sensitive issues associated with the research and the potentially low literacy levels of some of the research participants. The methodologies used to collect data include:

(1) *Dream trees.* A process by which children express their perspectives on issues important to them through pictorial representation.
(2) *Transect walks.* Ethnographic research conducted through informal interviews in the target villages. Through this research method, children and village leaders are empowered to act as guides as they lead the researcher through their community. During the walk, open questions are asked such as: what they like/dislike about their community; places they feel safe/unsafe in their community; the frequency and kind of visitors who come to their village.
(3) *Person-to-person interviews.* Conventional interviews between a researcher and children/vulnerable participants represent a gross power imbalance. Consequently, the research data can be greatly skewed, with the research participants providing the answers they think the researcher wants. However, if the research participants are provided questions and interview each other, it reduces the likelihood of skewed results. The researcher adopts a fly-on-the-wall approach and records the answers.
(4) *Focus groups.* These were used in village contexts with members of remnant communities. The groups were established to investigate the consequences of migration on families, culture and the community. During the research phase of the project, more than 10 focus groups were conducted. Each group had up to 20 participants but most focus groups had on average 12 participants. These were conducted with youth, village leaders and with existing community groups. The youth members were part of the community development project.
(5) *Face-to-face interviews.* These were conducted with key stakeholders in the Thai language. They included village leaders, community representatives, elected leaders, NGO representatives from groups such as World Vision, World Concern, Tearfund UK, TEAR Australia, AusAID and Mekong Minority Foundation.
(6) *Itinerant ethnography.* This approach relies on anecdotal information recorded through informal conversations and talks. Casual conversations with people on buses, trains, in the marketplace and elsewhere are recorded and used to help fill knowledge gaps in research methods.

Research Context

Thailand is a multi-ethnic nation made up of six major ethnic minority groups: Karen, Hmong, Lahu, Akha, Mien and Lisu. In addition, Thailand is also home to several smaller ethnic minority communities including the Khamu, Htin, Lua, Lue and Mlabri. The last census conducted by Thailand's Tribal Research Institute (1995) found almost 700,000 tribal people live in Thailand. These people are dispersed in more than 3,500 villages. The tribal populations are divided into two main groups: low-hill/high-valley people and highland groups that live in the mountains at altitudes higher than 1,000 metres. These ethnic minority communities are based predominantly in the north and north-east and are referred to as *khon chao khaao* in the Thai language. This paper focuses on one of these ethnic groups: the Hmong. Nonetheless, in the three target villages that the research centres on, there are Mien and Khamu people as well. The research has been conducted in northern Thailand's Nan Province. It is one of Thailand's most sparsely populated and remote provinces and has a high proportion of tribal people. More than 25 per cent of Nan's tribal population of 65,673 are Hmong. The villages that form the basis of the research are Ban Tham, Ban Song Khwae and Ban Doi Tiew.

The three communities are well-established villages that have only been 'opened' to the outside world through paved road links in the past 10 years. Prior to that, they were relatively isolated with nominal migration occurring, usually to nearby communities. During the 1970s and 1980s, these villages were targeted by Communist guerrillas as recruiting grounds in an attempted insurgency against the Thai Government. The willingness of some Hmong to serve as Communist foot soldiers contributed to feelings of distrust between the Thai majority and Hmong minority. However, it was during this time that the Thai Government invested heavily in infrastructure projects in these remote communities, to aid development, but more importantly to defeat the Communist threat. McCaskill (1997) argues that the Thai Government invested in infrastructure as part of a modernisation theory of development. Community development worker Jaa Saelao says these road networks have made villages more accessible and have provided people in the communities with great opportunities to travel. He says:

> In the past the communities were very isolated and if you wanted to travel anywhere you had to walk. It would take two days just to get to the main town in the district. But now it is about a 40-minute drive and you could drive to Bangkok if you wanted to in about 12 hours. It is much easier for people to travel and also to visit other places. (Personal communication, 12 October 2008)

This highlights that, in these communities, migration has occurred, in part, because they have an increased capacity to migrate. Emmers *et al.* support this arguing that:

> Within regions this process is intensified as shorter distances, lower costs and cultural affinities act as positive pressures on directing transnational population flows. In most cases these transnational flows are voluntary. (2008: 59)

Each of the villages that form the basis of the research has experienced mass migration during the past five years. In at least one of these villages, several homes have been locked and boarded up, as whole families have left the village in search of work as labourers in Bangkok. The initial act to leave these villages is often voluntary, but this migration can sometimes lead to issues of labour exploitation and trafficking, particularly among adolescents who leave their village communities.

Village Profiles

Ban Tham and Ban Song Khwae are located in Song Khwae district, Nan Province. The district's population is predominantly tribal with Hmong, Mien and Khamu the dominant tribal groups. Given the extensive border with Laos there is frequent cross-border activity for government-sanctioned markets each weekend. Beyond these official cross-border events however, there are also large numbers of itinerant people crossing the border, from Laos, into Song Khwae district. Ban Song Khwae is the district hub; a small village and administrative centre with government offices, a hospital and a high school. The village of Ban Tham is located less than 20 kilometres from Ban Song Khwae and is home to about 150 Hmong families. The residents of Ban Tham are generally classified as vulnerable by aid and community development agencies, with the average person surviving on less than AU$1 a day. Villagers grow seasonal crops such as corn and rice. Farmers with larger plots of land have invested in orange, mango and lychee orchards. In recent years, the village has faced a number of serious social issues including: a rapid increase in drug and substance abuse, an increase in the levels of pre-teen marriage and increasing levels of village-based violence. There have been increasing levels of migration from village teenagers travelling to either Ban Song Khwae or the provincial capital Nan City, to complete high school education. There have also been increasing levels of labour migration from people aged 20–40, who mostly travel to Bangkok in search of work opportunities to help financially support their families.

Ban Doi Tiew is located in Tha Wang Pha district, Nan Province. The village, located at an altitude of about 900 metres, is made up of mostly Hmong, however, some Mien families live on the outskirts of the village. This village of about 150 families has an approximate population of 1,800. The people in the villages are mainly farmers and grow crops such as rice, corn and lychees. Some families also raise cattle, thanks largely to intervention from a community development project operating in the village.

Following the construction of paved roads in recent years, more people have visited the village, as it is en route to a large National Park. These visitors are predominantly Thai and travel mainly during the winter months so they can experience a 'cold season'. Temperatures in the village plunge to near freezing during the peak cold months. The visitors sometimes seek to serve as recruitment agents, enticing people from the village to migrate to urban areas in search of more employment opportunities. Some of these opportunities are legitimate, but others are a front for organised crime gangs who traffic people into exploitative situations. In addition, other 'outsiders' seek to provide loans to villagers in seemingly acts of goodwill, so that villagers can buy seed for crops, support their children to obtain an education or simply to buy food. However, villagers have claimed that if these loans are not repaid, the loan sharks seek retribution, which can sometimes include the forced migration of indebted family members into exploitative situations in urban areas. This is seen as a method of debt repayment (personal communication, 17 August 2007).

Ban Doi Tiew village elder Xu Saelao said: "Hmong culture [is] changing, young people [are] leaving the village and never returning. Families are breaking down and the village has become a centre for drug and alcohol abuse" (Downman 2008: 23). The two main types of migration are: people leaving the village in search of work in urban areas or teenagers leaving the village to complete high school in other towns near the village.

Traditional Customs and Demographics of the Hmong

Hmong villages are among the most densely populated in Thailand. Hmong traditionally have large families and anecdotal evidence suggests Hmong are the fastest growing tribal group, in terms of population, in Thailand today. The average number of people in a Hmong household is eight, but it is not unusual for a family to have as many as 15 children (Lewis and Lewis 1998). Lewis and Lewis argue that the Hmong are among the most industrious of Thailand's tribal groups and seek economic independence as a means of advancing their quality of life (1998: 10). This enterprising vision, would explain in part, why Hmong communities have been so responsive to labour migration within Thailand. Beyond this industriousness, the Hmong are also associated with close family ties, with the family unit serving as the most important social unit. A family unit is usually made up of parents, their unmarried children, their married sons, their wives and children. It has been argued that the leader of the family is the most powerful and influential member of the Hmong community (Downman 2004: 143). Hence, when this unit starts to break down, there will inevitably be consequences for the broader community. Hmong communities are also divided into clans, represented by a clan name and an ancestral lineage. The highest level of social structure for Hmong is the community (*naiv neeg Hmong*), which is characterised by the notion of the collective and desire for a supportive and strong society.

In each level of Hmong society, men traditionally hold the leadership positions, but in recent years, there have been examples of women taking on leadership roles, particularly at a family level. Pao (1997) argues:

> [The leader] can create, maintain or destroy the reputation of his members. In general, it is fair to say the stronger the leader, the better the group will become. Conversely, the family with no leader or a weak leader is more likely to be scattered, have a low profile, face more challenges and the family's standing in the Hmong community may become mediocre.

It has been argued that to be Hmong involves participating effectively within a set social order (Downman 2004: 146). However, when external elements such as migration become a major factor within a Hmong community, upholding these traditional values and ideals not only becomes impossible but also serves to create a void that damages the community. McCaskill argues:

> Traditional indigenous culture differs significantly from the values, norms and practices that prevail in development and modernisation ... What is important for indigenous peoples in this context is that the processes of development and modernisation tend to destroy traditional culture. (1997: 28)

McCaskill argues that indigenous culture is more than traits, customs and rules, but includes a framework for people to express themselves and to embody a worldview. When this is altered in any significant way, it is disempowering, confusing and destructive to these communities.

Research Findings

The three communities that formed the basis of this research demonstrated three forms of migration: seasonal/contract migration, situational migration or permanent migration. Seasonal migration is typically associated with male workers migrating to another area of Thailand for a finite period usually in the field of agricultural production. There were however, instances of seasonal employment involving temporary migration to the USA or France. This pre-arranged overseas employment was normally facilitated by family members who had achieved refugee status in a third country and involved work in mainly family-run restaurants for periods of up to six months. During this time, villagers earn an income in euros or US dollars before returning to their village of origin. Situational migration typically applied to adolescents and children and was normally associated with migration for schooling or other types of education. Permanent migration was by far the most prevalent form of migration in the research sample, usually involving people, travelling large distances from their village of origin and only returning one or two times a year. During this time, they base themselves in another location with the primary goal of financially supporting the remnant family members in the village of origin. In the research sample, this typically involved both parents moving to Bangkok, where they were employed in a variety of industries including construction, retail, taxi driving or low-skilled occupations such as cleaning. In these instances, it was not unusual for spouses to separate and to live in different cities in search of higher paying work. In instances where the couple had children, they were typically left in the care of grandparents, other extended family members such as aunts or uncles or in some instances in the care of the oldest sibling. Village leaders said the migration of parents from villages had produced three main consequences in villages: a breakdown of traditional family values; drug and substance abuse; and suicide. Each of these issues will now be addressed.

Breakdown of Traditional Family Values

The three villages in the research revealed that migration had created a variety of complex social and cultural issues. These complexities had stemmed largely from the breakdown of traditional family values. Village leaders in each of the communities said that an absence of a 'generation of parents' meant that the traditional leadership roles within the family unit had either fallen into the hands of other children or the elderly, many of whom were too incapacitated or unwell to adequately meet the leadership needs of the family. One village leader in Ban Song Khwae said the consequences of migration had had a twofold impact on their community. He said that the community had lost many people to work in the city, but that outlying villages without high schools were sending teenage students to the village so that they could receive an education. He says:

> We had two impacts. We had families breaking down in the village because of migration and then all these kids turned up in the village. The parents from the outlying villages got together and rented them houses and in some houses there were 15 students living together without one adult. The parents said they wanted their children to go to high school and get an education but the children rarely went to school and caused problems in the community. It was a complete breakdown of the family responsibility. (Personal communication, 30 May 2008)

The village leaders said that many people saw migration as a panacea but were oblivious to the social effects that were occurring in the communities they were migrating from; because they felt they were acting in the best interest of the family, they did not realise the problems that were occurring with regard to family decision-making and family discipline. Research participants in each village said the problems with parents migrating from the village started about 10 years ago but had escalated during the past five years (Downman 2008). They said that there was now a generation of young people in the village that had grown up without parents. Xu Saelao said: "Young people are leaving for a job in Bangkok or the city. Sometimes they come back once a year for a visit, but sometimes they never come back" (Downman 2008: 23). Of Xu's nine children only four continue to live in the village, but he said he knew of some elderly residents who were now living in the village alone. Jaa Saelao said this 'neglect' of the elderly was unimaginable when he was growing up but had now become a reality for many of the village elders. He says:

> Hmong traditionally have lots of children so that as they get older there will be people around to look after them and take care of them. But high levels of migration mean that some old people now have no one to look after them. For those who are unwell, they must rely on the goodwill of others to care for them, feed them and provide them but there are no guarantees. (Personal communication, 14 February 2008)

This 'change' in family responsibility has created enormous social issues in villages with regard to care for the elderly. With no formal institutionalised care, and with villagers too poor to afford it even if it did exist, the elderly who remain in villages now face challenges of homelessness, poverty, malnutrition and death. Village elder Xu Saelao says: "His heart is sad because he sees Hmong culture changing, young people leaving the village and never returning" (Downman 2008: 23). He says that as a consequence of migration, the viability of village communities is under threat. Community development organisations such as TEAR Australia and Mekong Minority Foundation confirm that the sustainability of these communities is under threat. Director of Mekong Minority Foundation Scott Coats says that without intervention and sound development practices, these communities will cease to exist if current rates of migration continue. According to Coats, every family in these communities is affected and the consequences to the culture and quality of life are immense. He argues:

> It's a paradox because people are leaving the village, in most cases, to earn money and to have a better life and to share that with the family who remain in the village. Sometimes it works and there are success stories but most of the time there is pain and suffering not only for the person who has migrated but also for the family left behind. In rural Thailand it is an epidemic that is having tragic impacts on sending communities. (Personal communication, 30 April 2009)

The impacts on children are also great with deaths from preventable causes in recent years. Jaa Sae Lao said that in Ban Doi Tiew up to five children under the age of five disappeared every year believed to be mauled to death by dogs. He says this is because there is often no one to care for the children who may be playing outside, or wander into the jungle, and that the risks for children were very high (personal communication, 6 December 2008). He says:

> When you have children looking after children it will always cause problems. It's not unusual for a six or seven-year-old to be caring for younger children. This puts great pressure on them and they are not mature enough for these responsibilities. Children are mauled by dogs, burnt in fires or drown because of this. (Personal communication, 6 December 2008)

Because the family unit is the pivotal unit in Hmong culture these breakdowns within the traditional family structure are not only impacting the immediate families, but there are great spillover effects to clans and to the community at large.

Drug and Substance Abuse

Village leaders said that increasing levels of family dysfunction had important spillover effects for villages, with increasing levels of drug use and trafficking one of the worst outcomes. They said that because the traditional family unit had often collapsed, young people in village communities felt alienated and lost. In Ban Tham, there was increasing levels of substance abuse with teenage boys addicted to sniffing industrial strength glues. A village leader said that young people had become aware of glue sniffing after people who had migrated to Bangkok, shared stories of glue sniffing upon their return to the village. They said some had also seen glue sniffing on television (personal communication, 14 March 2009). Community development worker Jaa Sae Lao said local village leaders had met with shop owners in a nearby town, where youth went to buy the glue, and a ban was put in place preventing youth from buying it. He said:

> In the past families would work the fields together and be involved in traditional activities such as playing traditional games but now the youth have no interest in traditional culture or events. Their parents have not been around to pass on the traditions and they want to be more Thai than they do Hmong. Through the break up of families there has been a loss of values and a loss of their identity. (Personal communication, 9 January 2009)

Village leaders said that traditionally young people would be engaged in growing crops and learning about becoming leaders within their community, but because their income was now coming from relatives living in other places, there was less desire to be involved in traditional agriculture and that boredom and hopelessness were key issues for adolescents. One village leader from Ban Tham said communities were holding meetings regularly with elders concerned about the behaviour of youth, but that people felt powerless to act and were unaware of how to address issues of drug and substance abuse. He said there had been an increase in the use and sale of opium, smuggled into the village from Laos, and that villages like Ban Tham had become centres for drug use. Xu Saelao said in Ban Doi Tiew, people from nearby towns come to the village to use opium or amphetamines before driving home. He argues that because there are no police in villages, drug users believe there is less chance of being caught if drugs are used there. He argues that because many community role models have migrated from the village, there are no longer people to serve as the voice of reason to troubled youth. Village leaders in the three villages studied all identified increasing drug use as a major issue. Although they recognised it could not be tied solely to migration, they acknowledged that losing people to the city had contributed to the problem.

Suicide

The last significant issue in the three target communities linked to migration was suicide. The link between migration and suicide was twofold. Village leaders said that some people who had migrated to work in construction sites in Bangkok or in other countries often worked long hours, lived in poor accommodation and were treated poorly. One village leader in Ban Song Khwae said if these people return they are often scarred for life. He says:

We have seen this many times. They come back and they are not the same people. They don't talk to anyone and they might be addicted to alcohol or drugs. It is not unusual for them to take their own lives. After that there will often be a spate of suicides in the village and it's hard to know why. (Personal communication, 14 September 2008)

Jaa Sae Lao said in Ban Doi Tiew there were seven cases of suicide in 2008. He says most were young men who were part of the remnant community who had had family migrate from the village. He says:

A lot of them feel very alone and isolated. They have lost people from their family and their whole world has caved in. They might not have work in the village and they feel worthless. The culture has changed and they don't know how to respond. I have had men show me this plant that grows in the mountains. They told me that if you pick it and boil it and drink the water it will kill you very quickly. You go to sleep and you don't wake. Many people have told me they think this is a good idea and there seems to be a pattern. Others who miss their families just drink pesticide to take their own life. It is a major problem and there are direct links to migration. (Personal communication, 14 February 2009)

There are no official Thai government statistics on the rates of suicide in these communities but village leaders say the problem had increased rapidly in the past five years. Youth at a camp in Ban Tham in September 2008 said that suicide was an option most young people considered. One teenage participant said:

We have seen people go away and they've come back different people. Life here for us is very hard and then when we see people try and they fail and it doesn't give us much hope. Some of us don't have our parents and that makes us sad. We know why they have gone but we have lots of responsibilities. It's very hard. The world is very hard. Life here is very hard. (Personal communication, 14 September 2008)

Conclusion

Village-based issues are complex. It is difficult to blame one issue for a raft of problems in any community. However, it is clear that migration in Thailand's tribal communities has had a massive impact on families. This in turn has challenged cultural norms, which has affected whole communities as they grapple with un-precedented population shifts, declines and changes to the way their communities function. This has resulted in issues such as youth-based violence, drug and substance abuse, aged and childcare issues and increasing levels of suicide. This research presents anecdotal qualitative data, and greater quantitative research is needed to further document numbers of people migrating from villages. This preliminary research, however, supports Lyttleton's Lao-based findings (2005) that rural and regional communities are enduring complex 'social suffering' as a direct result of migration issues and that this has resulted in issues of drug abuse, vulnerability to HIV infection and mental health issues. It could also be concluded that regardless of whether migration from communities is international or domestic, migration has far-reaching consequences on remnant communities. Although much of the research to date, such as Castle's volume on ethnicity and globalisation (2000), has focused on macro approaches regarding this phenomenon it is clear that further micro research in remnant communities is needed to gauge the true extent of the issues created by migration. This research also supports Lüscher and Pillemer's argument (1998) that insufficient attention has been paid to the role of social change in this field of research. It is also clear that migration not only has tremendous impact on the social but also the traditional cultures of communities that have suffered as a consequence of migration.

This research in Nan, Thailand, has highlighted that migration has profoundly impacted the viability of these tribal communities. It has shown that the lives of the vulnerable in communities – children and the elderly – are now at great risk and that unless issues are addressed by communities, provincial and national governments and external development agencies, the viability and future of these villages, as well as their traditional cultural values, will be threatened.

Works Cited

Castles, S., 2000. *Ethnicity and globalization – from migrant worker to transnational citizen.* London: Sage.

de Haan, A., 2006. Migration, gender, poverty: family as the missing link? *In:* S. Arya and A. Roys, eds. *Poverty, gender and migration.* New Delhi: Sage, 107–128.

Downman, S., 2004. *Intra-ethnic conflict and the Hmong in Australia and Thailand.* Unpublished PhD thesis.

Downman, S., 2008. Mekong Minority Foundation: Part 3. *Target,* 3, 22–23.

Emmers, R., Greener, B.K. and Thomas, N., 2008. Securitising human trafficking in the Asia-Pacific: regional organisations and response challenges. *In:* M. Curley and S. Wong eds., *Security and migration in Asia: The dynamics of securitisation.* London: Routledge, 59–82.

Haseman, B., 2006. A manifesto for performative research. *Media international Australia,* 118, 98–106.

Lewis, P. and Lewis, E., 1998. *Peoples of the Golden Triangle.* London: Thames and Hudson.

Lüscher, K. and Pillemer, K., 1998. Intergenerational ambivalence. A new approach to the study of parent–child relations in later life. *Journal of marriage and the family,* 60 (2), 413–425.

Lyttleton, C., 2004. Relative pleasures: drugs, development and enduring dependencies in the Golden Triangle. *Development & change,* 35 (5), 909–935.

Lyttleton, C., 2005. Market bound – relocation and disjunction in northwest Laos. *In:* S. Jatrana, M. Toyota and B. Yeoh, eds. *Migration and health in Asia.* New York: Routledge, 41–60.

McCaskill, D., 1997. From tribal peoples to ethnic minorities: the transformation of indigenous peoples: a theoretical discussion. *In:* D. McCaskill and K. Kampe, eds. *Development or domestication? Indigenous peoples of Southeast Asia.* Chiang Mai: Silkworm Books, 26–60.

McCaskill, D. and Kampe, K., eds., 1997. *Development or domestication? Indigenous peoples of Southeast Asia.* Chiang Mai: Silkworm Books.

Pao, Saykao, 1997. *Hmong leadership: the traditional model.* Available from: www.hmongnet.org/hmong-au/leader [Accessed 15 August 2002].

Schloenhardt, A., 2008. Illegal migration and migrant smuggling in the Asia-Pacific: balancing regional security and human rights. *In*: M. Curley and S. Wong, eds. *Security and migration in Asia – the dynamics of securitisation.* London: Routledge, 35–56.

Teo, P., Graham, E., Yeoh, B. and Levy, S., 2003. Values, change and intergenerational ties between two generations of women in Singapore. *Ageing & society,* 23, 327–347.

Human Trafficking and Sex Industry: Does Ethnicity and Race Matter?

Natividad Gutiérrez Chong

In this article, I argue that racial and ethnic women are likely exposed to trafficking due to (1) structural poverty and marginalisation and (2) sexual violence is a common fact in domestic and social realms of socially excluded women and men. Racism affects women differently than men. The coinage of 'ethnosexuality' by Joane Nagel is indeed useful, as sex and sexuality are not detached from the social and cultural implications of race, racism and nationalism. My own scholarly interest in nationalism (state building and nation formation) has led me to turn towards racism and ethnicity and by looking at the empirical ground of such concepts these are constructed symbolically and objectively with sexuality. In the light of the evidence gathered, the following themes are interrelated: racist and sexist stereotypes of women are used in the sex industry; traditional patriarchal culture plays a role in reproducing female passivity and submission; racialised and ethnicised groups are prone to experience violence in all its forms, sexual exploitation being one of them.

There is nothing new about the notion that racism affects women in a different way than it does men. The former Human Rights High Commissioner Mary Robinson

(1997–2002) underlined the importance of providing special attention to three groups of women: refugees, victims of illegal trafficking and immigrants. These three groups are not alienated or detached from racism and discrimination; on the contrary, because they belong and/or reproduce ethnic and racial identity they are exposed to marginalisation and social alienation, which lead to further exploitation.

Below are some of Mary Robinson's observations:

- Discriminatory practices and exploitation affect women in disadvantageous communities.
- Race and ethnicity may be a factor of economic struggle in the trafficking of women, and that woman of certain racial and ethnic groups, indigenous and immigrants are much more vulnerable to trafficking, forced labour and slavery.
- The majority of woman of racial groups with disadvantages are living in poverty and the privatisation of health, in some countries, gives them limited access to these services.
- During armed conflicts, the rise of violence based on race and ethnicity is common, resulting in systematic rape, forced pregnancies, forced abortions, sexual abuse, sexual slavery and other serious human rights violations (Naciones Unidas n.d.).

Lydia Cacho, a Mexican journalist and human rights activist published in 2010, *Esclavas del poder. Un viaje al corazón de la trata sexual de mujeres y niñas en el mundo*. As a result of intense travels in Mexico and abroad, she presents a 'map of contemporary slavery' based on testimonies, interviews and her own observations. Why do men have to pay for sex and why do they have preferences for certain women? Such preferences imply that human trafficking is selective, that is, why I read her book as a journey, plagued with vivid conflicts of race, ethnicity and nationality, all interwoven with the suffering of girls and women from the global market throughout the Middle East, Asia, Africa and the Americas.

Various factors have to be considered in any study of human trafficking. First, 'The International Labor Organization (ILO) estimates that there are at least 2.4 million people in the process of being trafficked at any given moment generating profits as high as $32 billion (USD)' (Sun and Siskin 2010). Each year nearly four million women are sold for prostitution, slavery and/or forced marriages. Second, trafficking and smuggling are two of the many activities of organised crime, which is also linked with gang activity, illicit trade and corrupt authorities. Third, corruption is rampant at every level and not just among authorities; police, civil servants, federal agents, smugglers and bar owners all enslave and exacerbate sexual violence against women, which is indispensable to create an ambience of intimidation and harassment. Fourth, research is incipient; there are qualitative data available from testimonies and interviews, but no information on statistics or demographic data. Fifth, international legislation is available, such as the Convention for the Suppression of the Traffic in Persons and of the Exploitation of the Prostitution of Others (Dirección General de Compilación y Consulta del Orden Jurídico Nacional n.d.); Protocol to Prevent, Suppress and Punish Trafficking in Persons, especially Women and Children, supplementing the United

Nations Convention against Transnational Organized Crime (Office of the United Nations High Commissioner for Human Rights 2000); In Mexico, the General Law on the Prevention, Punishment and Eradication of Crimes on Trafficking in Persons and for the protection and assistance to victims of these crimes (Cámara de Diputados n.d.). Sixth, international efforts and campaigns aiming at preventing human trafficking is one of the new challenges of the globalised world (United Nations Office on Drugs and Crime 2004; United Nations General Assembly, 1993).

My objective in this paper is to explore whether race and ethnicity as a signpost of distinctive collective identities play a role in favouring the trafficking of women for the sex industry. My argument is that the social classification of women based on the construction of their racial and ethnic identities as non-dominant, which is also categorised by the hegemonic ideology and discourse as inferior, plays a major role in exposing them to trafficking, due to structural poverty and marginalisation, and to sexual violence, which is a common factor in the domestic and social realm that works to socially alienate them.

In light of the evidence gathered, the following themes are interrelated: racist and sexual stereotypes of women are exploited in the sex industry; traditional patriarchal culture has an idiosyncratic role in setting up stereotyped female passivity and submissiveness of the female attitude; racialised and ethnicised peoples are prone to experience violence in all its manifestations, sexual exploitation being one of them.

This article is structured in the following way. The first section mainly serves as a theoretical clarification of the main concepts involved, while the second provides a broad empirical background consisting of various cases in which race and ethnicity play a major role for choosing women for the sex industry. The empirical background is elaborated from a collection of stories gathered from multiple sources using different research techniques. Mexico is a case in point for providing some examples discussed here; however, other cases from all over the world were added to illustrate the importance of indicators of race and ethnicity in the global sex market.

This methodological approach will support the objective of developing a substantial reflection on the main aspects of the sociocultural phenomena stemming from the intersections of ethnicity and race in the trafficking of women for the sex industry. The analysis will embrace a global as well as a local perspective in the context of the contemporary circulations of symbols, goods and people within neoliberal capitalism and global migrations. Such a broad-gauge approach will contribute to understand the main aspects of this extended, transnational phenomenon, which requires to be studied from a comprehensive perspective that casts light into the tensions and flows between its global and its local constitutive traits.

Concepts

Racism, Race and Ethnicity

Racism is a set of beliefs and practices constructed around the physical differences of the human body. As an ideology, it becomes relevant because it categorises social groups and exerts a different social treatment according to scales (Telles 2004: 21). The ideology of racism works as an agent to justify abuse, lack of prestige, ridicule, negligence and rejection. In Mexico, both popular and scientific discourses neglect to refer to race as an agent for differentiation and segregation, the discourse of mixed race (miscegenation) or *mestizaje* provides the context of national unity, at the expense of rejecting and/or neglecting the cultural visibility of indigenous people and people of African background. Since ethnicity is not interchangeable with race, I prefer to discuss such a concept within the wide field of culture. Namely, the dominant discourse refers to ethnicity as belonging to an inferior culture because the reproduction of features of identity, such as indigenous languages, native origin, rural origin, ethnic ancestry and the safeguard of native cultures are often regarded as markers of underdevelopment or backwardness. According to Van Dijk (2003: 100), racism in Mexico (and Latin America) has obeisance to the European type of racism such as: skin, eye and hair colour, also size and stature are highly appreciated, and the less white a person is or the less blue or green eyed and/or short, the more likely he or she will be exposed to racism and this permits discrimination and abuse. Over the years, the conjugation of grades of skin colour and the negation of non-European culture have created a powerful stigmatisation of indigenous and Afro-descendant women, thus racism and ethnicity are ideologies expressed in various forms of violence, one being symbolic. Symbolic violence (Bourdieu 1977, 1998) is cultural but invisible constructions, as opposed to physical violence, which is exercised with the compliance of those who do not know, are being subject to it, and also when they themselves exercise it. Institutions and the media fabricate symbolic violence; it shows disparate ethnic and racial overtones and controls and manipulates sexuality. Race and ethnicity imprint women's lives and their social roles.

In that context, the coining of the concept 'ethnosexuality' by Joane Nagel (2003) in her thorough and fascinating book, *Race, Ethnicity and Sexuality. Intimate Intersections, Forbidden Frontiers*, is indeed a useful tool of analysis. Since sex and sexuality are not detached from the social and cultural implications of race, racism and nationalism:

> Ethnosexual frontiers are the borderlands on either side of ethnic divides; they skirt the edges of ethnic communities; they constitute symbolic and physical sensual spaces where sexual imaginings and sexual contact occur between members of different racial, ethnic and national groups. (Nagel 2003: 14)

My own scholarly interest of nationalism (state building and nation formation) has led me to turn towards racism and ethnicity and to look at the empirical ground of such concepts constructed symbolically and objectively with sexuality as a modern day commodity. Thus, in this article I will contend, using various stereotypical examples from media, popular literature, case studies and testimonies, that race and ethnicity play an important role in trafficking of women for the sex industry, not only in Mexico but also all over the world.

Race, ethnicity and the nationality of women sold to the sex trade offer a myriad of scenarios. Demand correlates with the fabrication of sexist stereotypes based on race and ethnic origin. Male consumption of prostitution reconfirms the correlation, as revealed by Janice G. Raymond *et al.* (2011). Paying for women from different races and nationalities, in many different ways, gives men the illusion of experiencing the 'exotic'. Male consumers do not ignore or underestimate a woman's race or ethnic identity and it is often an indicator for choosing. Again, Nagel (2003: 55) convincingly clarifies this discussion using the concept of 'ethnonosexual frontier' referred to as 'exotic, but volatile social spaces, fertile sites for the eruption of violence [...]. Both positive and negative stereotypes about the sexuality of ethnic Others reinforce ethnic differences and sustain ethnic segregation'. Finally, Nagel (2003: 56) adds: 'The sexual ideologies of both heterosexuals and homosexuals contain similar racialised images and stereotypes of erotic others: the sexual anxieties of white men, the sexual submissiveness of Asian woman, the sexual looseness of white woman, the sexual potency of black men'.

Race and ethnicity are social constructions and in the process the imagination of the popular and of the elite has created countless stereotypes that permeate all aspects of life. Stereotypes and archetypes realistically describe 'something' or 'someone' aiming at contributing to establish frontiers and differentiations between 'us' and 'them' within the context of daily life and routine, this way they remain solid but still, and above all banal. Archetypes are models of perfection, virtue or beauty that deserve admiration and even imitation; they range from heroes to impressive architecture to natural landscapes. On the other end, stereotypes are fixed and static attributes imposed arbitrarily by others to address 'someone' or 'something'. A noteworthy characteristic of stereotypes is that they forge fixed and static ideas to describe others and by doing so, a predictable outcome is expected and carries the weight of prejudices and contempt from one social group to the others (Gutiérrez 1998).

Latin America, with its inheritance of the colonial 'caste system', continues the tradition of the degraded stereotypes based on racialised groups of women, such as 'the black women for cleaning, the mulatto women for bedding and the white woman for marrying'. As this popular saying verifies, in Mexican society, there is a correlation expressed by 'class-race-ethnicity' combined with sexism and male domination, making poor indigenous and black women more exposed to an even deeper stage of discrimination. Historically, these women have experienced violence, denial of their basic human rights, ridicule, and are forced to remain silent and not to complain or make their grievances known. It is common for fear and shame to play a dominating factor in the lives of these women. And those conditions of symbolic domination and exploitation make them an easy target for their commercialisation in the sex industry.

If ethnic and racial markers are neglected in official records, we can observe in the sex industry a vast source for the exploitation of explicit racial and ethnic stereotypes. Precisely, one of the many sources that shows evidence of said stereotypes is to be found in films and popular literature – comics, cartoon strips, video games, advertising, and so on.

Human Trafficking

Human trafficking, which is also conceptualised as 'modern day slavery' (Lobasz 2009), is a complex phenomenon and a contested conceptual framing (Chuang 1998; GAATW 2000, 2006), as well as a geopolitical issue that may also vary according to state definitions of trafficking crimes and trafficking victims (Aromaa 2007): involving policy-making perspectives, law enforcement debates, the differing legal status of sex work/prostitution in different locations, human rights protection claims and intra-state and transnational migration flows. The notions of human trafficking are rooted on the specific political contexts in which it is framed. For the purposes of this article, therefore, which focuses on the intersections and convergences between human trafficking and the social constructions of race and ethnicity from a gender perspective, the notion of human trafficking will be drawn from and build on the UN international governance scope, as well as from a postcolonial, feminist critical framework.

According to the UN Protocol to Prevent, Suppress and Punish Trafficking in Persons trafficking is defined as:

> [...] the recruitment, transportation, transfer, harbouring or receipt of persons, by means of the threat or use of force or other forms of coercion, of abduction, of fraud, of deception, of the abuse of power or of a position of vulnerability or of the giving or receiving of payments or benefits to achieve the consent of a person having control over another person, for the purpose of exploitation. Exploitation shall include, at a minimum, the exploitation of the prostitution of others or other forms of sexual exploitation, forced labour or services, slavery or practices similar to slavery, servitude or the removal of organs. (United Nations Office on Drugs and Crime 2004, article 3, paragraph a)

Human trafficking is not a single event happening in a single moment (UNHCR 2006); it is, rather, a process within and/or across national borders that encompasses a set of diverse, entwined actions, involving specific acts achieved through particular means for the purpose of exploitation (United Nations Office on Drugs and Crime 2004).

From the traditional political and judicial perspective of the nation state, human trafficking is a national security issue, and represents a treat to sovereignty in terms of border control and law enforcement (Kempadoo 2005; Lobasz 2009, 2012) posed by transnational organised crime. Under this view, human trafficking is (or may be) a complementary activity within the chain of illegal businesses – such as drug and weapons trafficking or money laundering – carried out by international organised and/or discrete criminal associations and even small-scale operating individuals. Trafficking is indeed a criminal practice; therefore, correctly identifying its actors, agents and mechanisms is a matter of crucial importance (Sanghera 2005). Feminist activists and scholars as well as other human rights advocates are challenging, under ethical and efficacy arguments, the political precepts of national security (such as border reinforcement and victim repatriation) regarding trafficking prevention and protection.

Privileging the state's traditional security approach and the traditional law enforcement/'war-on-crime' fighting tools over the human rights perspective turns into an inefficient and unethical strategy to successful prevention and protection of the victims of human trafficking (Kempadoo 2005; Lobasz 2012). Trafficking is a violation of the victim's human rights and, according to the international laws, states have the obligation to prevent human rights abuses. It is still a common treatment for trafficked victims in general, and especially for women in prostitution cases, to be treated as criminals, therefore, undergoing a double abuse: first by the traffickers and then by the host state (DeStefano 2007; Lobasz 2012).

The feminist approach not only shifts the focus and discourse from state security to the security of people – the human rights of the trafficked person, but the feminist perspective of trafficking also argues for the crucial importance of analysing the role of gender categories and gender stereotypes in trafficking practices and its prosecution (Lobasz 2009).

Based on their collective experience in the fight against human trafficking, and in consistency with the approaches of the international bodies and experts and with the definition proposed in the UN Trafficking Protocol, the Global Alliance Against Trafficking in Women, the International Human Rights Law Group and the Foundation Against Trafficking in Women (1999), in conjunction with various other non-governmental organisations (NGOs) worldwide, coined a definition of trafficking that privileges the human rights perspective over the criminal justice approach and emphasises the violence and coercive dimension inflicted upon people, involving:

> All acts and attempted acts involved in the recruitment, transportation within and across borders, purchase, sale, transfer, receipt or harbouring of a person involving the use of deception, coercion (including the use or threat of force or the abuse of authority) or debt bondage for the purposes of placing or holding such person, whether for pay or not, in servitude (domestic, sexual or reproductive), in forced or bonded labour, or in slavery like conditions, in a community other than the one in which such person lived at the time of the original deception, coercion or debt bondage. (Foundation against Trafficking in Women/International Human Rights Law Group/Global Alliance against Traffic in Women 1999)

In this regard, coercion can be manifested in various forms, including (though not limited to) violence and the threat of violence (Chew 1999: 14).

Violence

In the 1990s, after the intense lobbying of international NGOs at different levels, trafficking was included in the UN's human rights, population and women agendas, and was classified as a form of gender violence. The Declaration on the Elimination of Violence Against Women was adopted by the UN General Assembly in 1993 defines:

> violence against women' as 'any act of gender-based violence that results in, or is likely to result in, physical, sexual or psychological harm or suffering to women,

including threats of such acts, coercion or arbitrary deprivation of liberty, whether occurring in public or private life. (Art. 1)

The Declaration includes trafficking and forced prostitution practices as a form of violence against women (Art. 2-b), as well as 'Physical, sexual and psychological violence perpetrated or condoned by the State, wherever it occurs' (Art. 2-c).

Lin Chew suggests that this shift in international human rights policy towards gender inequities and violence awareness may reinforce the accountability of nation states regarding their efforts to suppress gender violence (1999: 11). For example, in 2008, the UN adopted two new resolutions related to violence against women; specifically, Resolution 63/156 (United Nations General Assembly 2009) focuses on trafficking in women and girls and urges governments to take appropriate actions in this regard.

Nevertheless, most of the legislation on these issues specifically addresses trafficking prostitution cases in transnational circumstances, leaving migrant women workers without proper legislation to protect them and grant them rights (Chew 1999: 11) against diverse forms of exploitation and, when prosecuted, evidence has shown that women victims of trafficking are criminalised, being more severely punished by state laws than their exploiters and /or violators (Chew 1999: 15).

Structural Poverty

The UN's Economic Commission for Latin America and the Caribbean (ECLAC) defines structural poverty as a situation in which an individual has one or more unsatisfied basic needs but is not income poor, and poses a territorial manifestation of the position occupied by the poor in the social structure (Kessler and de Virgilio 2008; ECLAC 2009). In what Pierre Sané, UNESCO's Assistant Director-General for the Social and Human Sciences Sector in 2006, describes as a vicious circle, poverty is a key interconnected factor in the socioeconomic scenarios of the human rights violations that comprise human trafficking, especially of women and children, particularly in migratory contexts, in turn, increasing deprivation, disadvantage and, once again, exploitation (Truong 2006: 7). From this perspective, human trafficking is a by-product of social global inequity. As Chang and Kim (2007) note, the global flows and polarisations among the national state centres of power that reinforce neoliberal economic policies and the developing regions, which are battered by factors such as impoverishment as well as civil and political instability, are all elements that facilitate trafficking and labour exploitation.

Recently, the broader social conditions of the communities where trafficking processes are present have been analysed considering the varying supply and demand factors that impact these practices (Truong 2006: 110). Authors, such as Chuang (2006: 137), propose 'to reframe trafficking as a migratory response to current globalising socioeconomic trends', urging analysts to assess the conditions of lack of access to basic necessities – such as the deprivation of elemental economic, social and cultural entitlements and rights in local contexts – that cause people to migrate under circumstances of high vulnerability. Discrimination plays an important role in this scenario, worsening the circumstances for women, who mostly lack access to legal migration channels and are relegated to the informal machineries of economic reproduction (Chuang 2006: 138, 140). Poverty, together with gender, sexual orientation, ethnic and race discrimination are underlying structural components in human trafficking.

Racist and Sex Stereotypes of Women Exploited in the Sex Industry

Black Women

Testimonies and all sorts of evidence portraying black women in stereotypical racist and sexist images are legendary. Some of these prejudices come from the colonial roots in the Americas, like their alleged promiscuity and eagerness for having sex 'Everything about African-American women is sexualized in pornography [...] Racist stereotypes in the mainstream media and in the porn industry portray black women as wild animals ready for any kind of sex, anytime and with anybody' (Stark and Whisnant 2004: 86).

A large majority of trafficked persons in the USA for purposes of labour and sexual exploitation are people of colour (non-white). According to the US Department of Justice, 50 per cent of trafficked victims are children and, in overwhelming numbers, girls. The Polaris Project estimates that about 17,500 victims of trafficking each year are mostly women, children and men from countries like Mexico and East Asia, as well as from South Asia, Central America, Africa and Europe (Polaris Project n.d.). According to statistics from the Bureau of Justice, 77 per cent of the alleged victims reported in the USA for incidents involving human trafficking were people of colour (Bureau of Justice Statistics n.d.). Young African women are also in a high demand in Europe. 'UNICEF estimates that between 60% and 80% of the girls involved in sex trade are Nigerians, with an average age of 15' (Onyejekwe 2005: 144). In present-day Italy, more than 60 per cent of sex workers come from rural Nigeria (*The Nigerian Voice* 2011). I recently found the following comment from an Argentinean blogger:

> I think that people associate my racial appearance with the rampant human trafficking that brings thousands of Dominicans, Brazilians and people of other nationalities, often to work as prostitutes. Unfortunately, for many here, being of African descent and a female is associated with prostitution and sexual slavery. (Mason 2008)

Indigenous Women

Indigenous women from the Americas endure higher rates of sexual violence than any other group, rooted in the ideological racist misogyny that portrays Indian women as 'unclean'. There is also a video game called 'Custer's Revenge', the aim of which is to score points by raping Native American women. Worldwide, 75 per cent of indigenous women have experienced a sexual assault, and native women of ethnic and racial origin have 2.5 times more likelihood of suffering a rape, and more than one of three indigenous women will be exposed to some kind of abuse in her lifetime (El Mundo 2007). The US Department of Justice states that 86 per cent of the men responsible for sexual violence towards ethnic native women who come from a non-indigenous backgrounds (Amnesty International 2007).

The current racist ideology combined with sexism focuses attention on the stereotypes of the 'passive, non-emancipated women from the developing world'. Patriarchy, globalisation and militarisation are also involved in the sex industry. US military bases press for young indigenous and aboriginal women from the Philippines and other Pacific Islands (Kuokkanen 2008, Moon 2008).

Historically, Central America has a high rate of human rights abuses, such as discrimination, violence against women and indigenous women, as well as human trafficking. One striking and horrifying aspect of this illicit activity is that it involves women as young as 12 years old. It is reported that more than 5,000 Central Americans are thrown into prostitution in various municipalities of the Southern Mexican border, particularly in bordellos along the Pan-American Highway.

For Central Americans, Mexico may represent the opportunity to reach the USA or be stuck in some town along the Mexican southern border. For these migrants, their available opportunities are to engage in domestic services or prostitution. According to Arun Kumar (2006), between 6,000 and 8,000 women are smuggled into Mexico. In the Southern city of Tapachula, Chiapas (on the border with Guatemala), 40 per cent of the sex workers aged 14–24 come from Guatemala, 35 per cent come from Honduras and 25 per cent from El Salvador.

From his fieldwork, Kumar also observes that 7 out of 10 women stayed in the Chiapas region and only 3 would move somewhere else. This is important as it reveals a high concentration of smuggled women to the southern border. Three factors may explain such numbers: first, the extreme surveillance of immigration agents and specialised police in the rest of Mexico, including the northern border, makes the transportation of women more difficult. It also makes the any attempt to take women away from the border, in case they need to escape or hide, more risky. Second, there is a growing demand for women in Mexico. Since 1994, the Mexican tourist industry has grown 5 times over. The sex industry has also expanded rapidly and it is still to be investigated if there are links between the high concentration of smuggled women and the growth of both tourism and sex industries. Third, a trafficked woman is more profitable if she remains in Mexico than if transported to the USA; the smuggler is able to exercise his power and domination over the woman more than once, he may ask for commissions or fees within the network (madam, bar owner, authorities).

Kumar's work on the smuggling of women in Tapachula recorded some interviews showing the purpose of trafficking: prostitution, forced labour and sexual violence. Consider a typical case of one of the woman interviewed, 'Paola': her case is representative as it reveals how a smuggler deceives, often in complicity with her father or another male family authority, under the promise of a well-paid job; to exert complete domination and control she is treated with violence and put under permanent threat; she had no freedom of action, a characteristic of modern slavery. She has accumulated debts and is under the strict surveillance of her guardians (Kumar 2007).

As mentioned above, retention of women in Mexico is a flourishing business. 'Paola's case' represents an example of some of the ideal characteristics requested of women. Age, as early as 9–25, and the physical appearance of the girl are also an important factor. Here, the discussion of ethnicity and race as a marker of indigenous women becomes important in the male consumption of the sex industry, and if we take the Spanish language as a case in point, it is estimated that most of the smuggled women from Guatemala (and Mexico) come from an indigenous origin and, therefore, have a limited command of the Spanish language. Non-Spanish proficiency lowers the price of a woman, because the members of the crime ring argue that she requires more investment on her training, which means that such a girl will be put up late in the sexual market and the investor will have to wait longer in collecting profits. Ethnicity lowers the price of a woman, but so too does her race, and those characteristics imply that they are more likely to be sold, but the ringleaders also take into consideration the women's skin colour: 'I earn very little money with indigenous women, because the bar owners do not find them attractive, mainly because of their dark skin' (Kumar 2006).

In the Norogachi region within the Tarahumara Sierra (Northern Mexico), indigenous young women from the Rarámuri ethnic identity said that they left their village under the false promise of a job in the city of Chihuahua, but in fact they were forced into prostitution, as described in local newspaper reports[1] (Volchanskaya 2005).

Let us now take a look into two final cases. The first case was from a study in New York, San Francisco and Minneapolis/St. Paul where men were asked to voluntarily write their preferences for female sex workers by downloading an Internet questionnaire (Raymond *et al.* 2011). The second case is an exploration of Mexican male preferences for sex consumption using popular literature – a massive entertainment in the form of comics or fictional small books or cartoon strips sold in Mexico City.

The Internet Questionnaire

In New York, San Francisco and Minneapolis/St. Paul, men were asked to voluntarily write their preferences about sex consumption by downloading an Internet questionnaire (Raymond *et al.* 2011).

Any form of collected data with neatly presented statistics for trafficked women is not available. Therefore, at least *two* methodological questions should be taken into consideration. First, all available data attempting to show the extent of trafficked women should be regarded as a useful preliminary tool for further research. Second, race and ethnic identity variables conflate into the grouping of races into black, white, and so on, but such conflation may not reflect the standard nationality or ethnic origin of women, for example, Korean, Laotian, Thai or Japanese are grouped under the Asian race, without reflecting the economic disparities of each nation.

Ukrainians, Russians and Polish are placed under the white category but serves as a disguise for the unprivileged and economic hardships of the Eastern Bloc, and within the black category we have women from Brazil, Nigeria and Colombia. By the same token, the Hispanic/Latin group may include women from Argentina, indigenous women from Central America or El Salvador. However, given the difficulty for gathering data, such information remains useful and it offers a general picture of the international trade of women in the USA.

The available evidence indicating that they do not speak the language of the host country can deduct that women are smuggled for the sex market worldwide. Again, the study by Carol J. Gomez and her colleagues provides useful insights:

> New York
> She was the only Brazilian in the place [...] She didn't speak a lot of English.
> She is from Argentina. I [...] tried to talk to her, but she hardly spoke any English.
> All of the women were Hispanic. Two of the girls could not even speak much English.
> San Francisco
> The staffs appear to be all Korean.
> The women range from stunning to plain, Korean to Vietnamese.
> Korean women [...] new immigrants – inexperienced.

According to the study mentioned, and I quote; 'One of the most significant findings is the greater number of women from South America in New York, and the greater number of Asian nationals in San Francisco' (Raymond *et al.* 2011).

Popular Literature

In order to explore whether female physical features can determine the consumption of male preferences, I studied samples of 15 titles of reading material for popular male consumption sold in newspapers stands in Mexico City. The methodology of the study implies that the stories, characters depicted and the use of language provided some clues for detecting if race and ethnicity played a role in the sex industry; therefore, I visited the distribution warehouses of said low-cost reading materials for massive consumption. The 15 titles were chosen at random, using the following criteria: cover, title, content and advertising. It is important to note that these types of reading material only depict fictional characters. The stories are mostly about Indians and cowboys, heroes, leaders, gangs and entrepreneurs. They all have the same 'romantic storyline' that usually takes place between the fictional female and male characters, so bodies, language, roles and wardrobe are merely an excuse of the imagination to exaggerate and manipulate the female body with broad hips and enormous breasts as a style of drawing. Some of the stories contain explicit sexual material in the narrative; the illustrations are drawings with colour, sepia or black and white. In contrast, the advertising pages are colourful photos that publish sex call centres or realistic sexual material. It is evident that all the women portrayed in the ad pages have the same physical features: white skin, blond or fair hair. There are no dark or ethnic women appearing in the ad pages. Although these pages are also illustrated with colour photographs of 'real women', the European characteristics of beauty of said photos, fair curly hair, fair eyes, fair skin, slim and tall, are evident. These women are portrayed as commodities not easy to reach; they advertise desirability on account of their fair skin and hair. By reading these cheap fictional stories, the male consumer may fantasise with the 'exoticism' of the fair skin. According to the owner of the warehouse, only men consume this type of material. The website of a highly popular reading material *El libro vaquero* ('The cowboy book') makes available some revealing statistics which help to draw the reader's profile: 40 per cent are workers or artisans, 60 per cent are aged 21–30, 40 per cent earn 2 to 4 times the minimum salaries, 72 per cent are male readers. These statistics are available as part of a marketing strategy aimed at selling publicity in the ad pages, given that *El libro vaquero* sells the amazing figure of 400,000 copies per week, since 1977. In short, young, unskilled, low-income males are regular buyers of fictitious stories who prefer fair-skinned women for sexual consumption (*Hevi Editores* n.d).

Traditional Patriarchal Culture Plays a Major Role in Portraying Female Passivity and Submission

Women who belong to highly traditional, patriarchal *macho* cultures have little or no background for defending themselves, making women more susceptible to violence and trafficking. Domesticity and traditional culture are contributing factors for indigenous women to become victims of the sex trade. Absolute obedience to a male and/or a husband is expected from indigenous women, and this carries a list of duties, such as remaining in silence and refraining from seeking help or refuge from the brutality of her male counterparts in the domestic environment or after in the sexual trade environment. It is expected from indigenous women that they take 'their secret to the grave' or to 'keep men's secrets forever'. They are discredited and distrusted and do not expect any justice since it is only a privilege for men, for the well-being of men only. Such is the cultural and traditional environment that does not allow women any chance to denounce her condition or eventual trafficking. Indigenous women also have cultural features that make them susceptible to oppression and harassment: they are not Spanish speakers, are mostly illiterate, submissive and obedient and are used to physical aggression and abuse and have a low self-esteem.

Conclusion: Racialised and Ethnicised Peoples are Prone to Experience Violence in All Its Manifestations, Sexual Exploitation Being One of Them

It is estimated that 70 million women in Latin America come from Afro and native indigenous backgrounds. Both race and ethnicity are the reasons for their poverty, illiteracy and social alienation. With no opportunities offered by the welfare state and its policies, these women have been historically engaged in low-profit activities and the informal economy and that kind of structure becomes fertile soil for further exploitation, whether trafficking or sexual abuse.

Women are at a disadvantage because of symbolic violence and structural poverty. Race and ethnicity contribute to those structural disadvantages and as a result women of black and indigenous background have to face extreme discrimination, racism and sexism. Discriminated women are subject to further exploitation by organised crime in trafficking and prostitution and these criminal organisations rely on women who are unable to defend themselves and become victims of control with the use of physical and psychological violence, intimidation and harassment. The hook to gain profit from discriminated women comes from deception, that is, false promises for a better life, and from their own folk that sells them to help the family to survive.

Ethnicity and race do matter in the following aspects: first, the exoticism of women, based on race or ethnicity, is a valuable asset in the market. The case of New York consumers – the exploitation of non-white women from around the globe, and the case of Mexico City – where the male preference is for white and blond women, that is, Mexican male readers seem to prefer white women. Second, unprivileged ethnicity and race cheapen the price of a woman. Indigenous women are smuggled with false promises of jobs which explain Central American indigenous women in Southern Mexico and the case of Rarámuri girls. These two cases illustrate the cultural and physical features associated with the inferiorised identity of an ethnic group. Third, sexual exploitation goes hand in hand with male domination and violence against women of a certain ethnic and racial background, that is, video games offering the rape of indigenous women as entertainment. Forth, structural poverty and social alienation affect mainly ethnic women and non-white women.

If gender policies and official programmes start to recognise the ethno-racial indicators in statistics with well-informed documentation, widespread attention to the plight of these women may help to identify the reasons for the sex trade and to put an end to it. States should revise the national legal ways to protect women against discrimination by race as Mary Robinson summoned more than a decade ago.

Acknowledgements

This article is part of the research project 'Racismo en la era del multiculturalismo' (IIS-UNAM). The author wishes to acknowledge the two anonymous evaluations that this article received. Many thanks to Luis Madáhuar for guiding me in the world of male consumption of popular literature and to Abeyami Ortega and Dalia Quiroz for their editorial advice.

Note

[1] Sophisticated practices of trafficking of women and adolescents have reached indigenous communities. Procurers from Chihuahua and Juárez are arriving to small villages in the Sierra to recruit young women under the promise of a job, but the real aim is to force them into prostitution. It happened in the Norogochi region, where eight young women return to their village and told what they were forced to do. It was denounced by Juan Gardea García, indigenous from Norogachi, Guachochi, who is also a State Coordinator of Tarahumara de la Coordinadora Estatal de la Tarahumara (Volchanskaya 2005, *My translation*).

Works Cited

Amnesty International, 2007. *Maze of injustice. The failure to protect indigenous women from sexual violence in the USA*. Available from: http://www.amnesty.org/en/library/asset/AMR51/035/2007/en/ce2336a3-d3ad-11dd-a329-2f46302a8cc6/amr510352007en.html [Accessed 23 October 2012].

Aromaa, K., 2007. Trafficking in human beings: uniform definitions for better measuring and for effective counter-measures. *In*: Savona and Stefanizzi, eds. *Measuring human trafficking: complexities and pitfalls*. New York: Springer, 13–36.

Bourdieu, P., 1977. Sur le pouvoir symbolique. *Annales. Économies, Sociétés, Civilisations*, 32 (3), 405–411. Available from: http://www.persee.fr/web/revues/home/prescript/article/ahess_0395-2649_1977_num_32_3_293828 [Accessed 13 December 2013].

Bourdieu, P., 1998. *La domination masculine*. Paris: Seuil.

Bureau of Justice Statistics, n.d. *Data collection: National Crime Victimization Survey (NCVS), Office of Justice Programs: U.S. Department of Justice*. Available from: http://bjs.ojp.usdoj.gov/index.cfm?ty=dcdetail&iid=245 [Accessed 23 October 2012].

Cacho, L., 2010. *Esclavas del poder. Un viaje al corazón de la trata sexual de mujeres y niñas en el mundo*. Mexico City: Grijalbo.

Cámara de Diputados, n.d. *Ley general para prevenir, sancionar y erradicar los delitos en materia de trata de personas y para la protección y asistencia a las víctimas de estos delitos*. Estados Unidos Mexicanos. Available from: http://www.diputados.gob.mx [Accessed 23 October 2012].

Chang, G. and Kim K., 2007. Reconceptualizing approaches to human trafficking: new directions and perspectives from the field(s). *Stanford journal of civil rights and civil liberties*, 3 (2)/ Loyola Law School, Legal Studies Paper No. 2007–47. Available from: http://papers.ssrn.com/sol3/papers.cfm?abstract_id=1051601 [Accessed 13 December 2013].

Chew, L., 1999. Global trafficking in women: some issues and strategies. *Women's studies quarterly*, 27 (1/2), 11–18.

Chuang, J., 1998. Redirecting the debate over trafficking in women: definitions, paradigms and contexts. *Harvard human rights journal*, 11, 65–108. Available from: http://traffickingroundtable.org/wp-content/uploads/2012/08/Redirecting-the-Debate-over-Trafficking-in-Women-Definitions-Paradigms-and-Contexts.pdf [Accessed 2 September 2013].

Chuang, J., 2006. Beyond a snapshot: preventing human trafficking in the global economy. *Indiana journal of global legal studies*, 13 (1), 137–163. Available from: http://www.repository.law.indiana.edu/cgi/viewcontent.cgi?article=1323&context=ijgls [Accessed 3 September 2013].

DeStefano, A., 2007. *The war on human trafficking: U.S. Policy Assessed*. New Brunswick, NJ: Rutgers University Press.

Dirección General de Compilación y Consulta del Orden Jurídico Nacional, n.d. *Convención Para La Represión De La Trata De Personas Y De La Explotación De La Prostitución Ajena*. Estados Unidos Mexicanos. Available from: http://www.ordenjuridico.gob.mx/TratInt/Derechos%20Humanos/D46.pdf [Accessed 23 October 2012].

Economic Commission for Latin America and the Caribbean (ECLAC), 2009. *Income poverty and unsatisfied basic needs. United Nations, ECLAC subregional headquarters Mexico.* Available from: http://www.eclac.org/publicaciones/xml/0/38190/L949.pdf [Accessed 8 September 2013].

El Mundo, 2007. EEUU no protege a las mujeres indígenas frente a los elevados índices de violación, *Elmundo.es,* 24 May. Available from: http://www.elmundo.es/elmundo/2007/04/24/solidaridad/1177422416.html [Accessed 23 October 2012].

Foundation against Trafficking in Women/International Human Rights Law Group/Global Alliance against Traffic in Women, 1999. *Human rights standards for the treatment of trafficked persons.* Bangkok: Global Alliance against Traffic in Women. Available from: http://gaatw.org/books_pdf/hrs_eng1.pdf [Accessed 2 September 2013].

Global Alliance against Traffic in Women (GAATW), 2000. *Human rights and trafficking in persons: A handbook.* Available from: http://www.ungift.org/docs/ungift/pdf/knowledge/Human%20Rights%20and%20Trafficking%20in%20Person.pdf [Accessed 2 September 2013].

Global Alliance against Traffic in Women (GAATW), 2006. Response by the Global Alliance Against Traffic in Women (GAATW) to the Report of the Special Rapporteur on trafficking in persons, especially women and children, Sigma Huda: Integration of the Human Rights of Women and the Gender Perspective, E/CN.4/2006/62, 20 February, 62nd Session of the Commission on Human Rights. Available from: http://www.gaatw.org/UNAdvocacy/GAAT-WResponseSigmaHuda%27sReport1.pdf [Accessed 2 September 2013].

Gutiérrez, C.N., 1998. Arquetipos y estereotipos en la construcción de la identidad nacional de México, Revista Mexicana de Sociología, año LX, núm. 1, enero-marzo, Instituto de Investigaciones Sociales, Universidad Nacional Autónoma de México.

Hevi Editores, n.d. *Perfil del lector.* Available from: http://hevi.mx/perfil.html [Accessed 23 October 2012].

Kempadoo, K., 2005. From moral panic to global justice: changing perspectives on trafficking. *In:* K. Kempadoo, J. Sanghera, and B. Pattanaik, eds. *Trafficking and prostitution reconsidered: new perspectives on migration, sex work, and human rights.* Boulder and London: Paradigm, vii-xxxiv.

Kessler, G. and de Virgilio, M.M., 2008. The new urban poverty: global, regional and Argentine dynamics during the last two decades. *CEPAL review,* 95 (August), 31–50. Available from: http://www.eclac.org/publicaciones/xml/0/34760/RVI95KesslerDiVirgilio.pdf [Accessed 15 August 2013].

Kumar, A., 2006. *La Esclavitud Humana: El tráfico de mujeres en la India y México, Facultad de Filosofía y Letras.* México, D.F: Tesis de doctorado. Instituto de Investigaciones Antropológicas, Universidad Nacional Autónoma de México.

Kumar, A., 2007. El mercado de las mujeres. Globalización, migración y tráfico de mujeres en México. *Trayectorias: Revista de Ciencias Sociales de la Universidad Autónoma de Nuevo León,* 23 (Enero–Abril), 9–17.

Kuokkanen, R., 2008. Globalization as racialized, sexualized violence. *International feminist journal of politics,* 10 (2), 216–233. Available from: http://rauna.files.wordpress.com/2008/05/793277480_content.pdf [Accessed 23 October 2012].

Lobasz, J., 2009. Beyond border security: feminist approaches to human trafficking. *Security studies,* 18 (2), 319–344.

Lobasz, J., 2012. *Victims, villains, and the virtuous constructing the problems of 'Human Trafficking'.* Dissertation (PhD). Graduate School of the University of Minnesota. June 2012. Available from: http://conservancy.umn.edu/bitstream/131822/1/Lobasz_umn_0130E_12756.pdf [Accessed 2 September 2013].

Mason, V., 2008. Human trafficking in Argentina and the world. *Subject to Change: Social Change from a public Health Perspective,* 14 September. Available from: http://vanessamason.wordpress.com/category/argentina/ [Accessed 23 October 2012].

Moon, K., 2008. Military prostitution and the U.S. Military in Asia. *The Asia-Pacific journal: Japan focus*. Available from: http://www.japanfocus.org/-Katharine_H_S_-Moon/3019 [Accessed 23 October 2012].

Naciones Unidas, n.d. *Alto Comisionado de los Derechos Humanos, Centro de Información*. Available from: http://www.cinu.org.mx/temas/dh/mello.htm [Accessed 23 October 2012].

Nagel, J., 2003. *Race, ethnicity and sexuality: Intimate intersections, forbidden frontiers*. New York: Oxford University Press.

Office of the United Nations High Commissioner for Human Rights, 2000. *Protocol to prevent, suppress and punish trafficking in persons especially women and children, supplementing the United Nations convention against transnational organized crime*. Available from: http://www.osce.org/odihr/19223 [Accessed 23 October 2012].

Onyejekwe, C., 2005. Influences of global human trafficking issues on Nigeria: A gender perspective. *Journal of international women's studies*, 7 (2), 141–151. Available from: http://vc.bridgew.edu/cgi/viewcontent.cgi?article=1439&context=jiws [Accessed 23 October 2012].

Polaris Project, n.d. *Sex trafficking in the U.S.* Available from: www.polarisproject.org/human-trafficking/sex-trafficking-in-the-us [Accessed 23 October 2012].

Raymond, J., Hughes, D. and Gómez C., 2011. *Sex trafficking of women in the United States*. Kingston: University of Rhode Island. Available from: http://www.uri.edu/artsci/wms/hughes/sex_traff_us.pdf [Accessed 23 October 2012].

Sanghera, J., 2005. Unpacking the trafficking discourse. *In*: K. Kempadoo, J. Sanghera, and B. Pattanaik, eds. *Trafficking and prostitution reconsidered: new perspectives on migration, sex work and human rights*. New Brunswick, NJ: Rutgers University Press, 3–24

Stark, C. and Whisnant, R. 2004. *Not for sale. Feminists resisting prostitution and pornography*. Melbourne: Spinifex Press.

Sun, L. and Siskin A., 2010. *Trafficking of people: US policy and issues for congress*. Congressional Research Service, 18 February. Available from: http://fpc.state.gov/documents/organization/139278.pdf [Accessed 23 October 2012].

Telles, E., 2004. *Race in another America: the significance of skin color in Brazil*. Princeton, NJ: Princeton University Press.

The Nigerian Voice, 2011. 60 percent of prostitutes in Italy are nigerians. *The Nigerian Voice*, 19 October. Available from http://www.thenigerianvoice.com/nvnews/72366/1/60-percent-of-prostitutes-in-italy-are-nigerians.html [Accessed 23 October 2012].

Truong, T.-D., 2006. *Poverty, gender and human trafficking in Sub-Saharan Africa: rethinking best practices in migration management*. Paris: UNESCO. Available from: http://us-cdn.creamermedia.co.za/assets/articles/attachments/02542_poverty1432e.pdf [Accessed 9 March 2013].

United Nations General Assembly, 1993. Declaration on the elimination of violence against women (A/RES/48/104), 20 December. Available from: http://www.un.org/documents/ga/res/48/a48r104.htm [Accessed 20 December 2013].

United Nations General Assembly, 2009. Resolution adopted by the General Assembly on the report of the Third Committee (A/63/425)] 63/156. Trafficking in women and girls. Available from: http://daccess-dds-ny.un.org/doc/UNDOC/GEN/N08/480/15/PDF/N0848015.pdf?OpenElement [Accessed 02 September 2013].

United Nations High Commission for Refugees (UNHCR), 2006. The Application of Article 1A (2) of the 1951 Convention and/or 1967 Protocol relating to the Status of Refugees to victims of trafficking and persons at risk of being trafficked (UNHCR Guidelines on International Protection 2006).

United Nations Office on Drugs and Crime, 2004. *United Nations convention against transnational organized crime and the protocols thereto*. New York. Available from: http://www.unodc.org/unodc/en/treaties/CTOC/ [Accessed 23 October 2012].

Van Dijk, Teun A. 2003. *Racismo y discurso de las elites*. Barcelona: Gedisa.

Volchanskaya, O., 2005. En Juárez y Chihuahua se recluta a mujeres indígenas para la prostitución. *El Diario*, 13 Junio. Available from: http://www.mujeresenred.net/spip.php?breve148 [Accessed 23 October 2012].

Index